SURVIVAL
of the
FITTEST
for
INVESTORS

USING DARWIN'S LAWS of EVOLUTION to BUILD a WINNING PORTFOLIO

DICK STOKEN

New York   Chicago   San Francisco   Lisbon   London
Madrid   Mexico City   Milan   New Delhi   San Juan
Seoul   Singapore   Sydney   Toronto

1 2 3 4 5 6 7 8 9 0   QFR/QFR   1 6 5 4 3 2 1

ISBN: 978-0-07-178228-9
MHID: 0-07-178228-1

e-ISBN: 978-0-07-178229-6
e-MHID: 0-07-178229-X

This publication is designed to provide accurate and authoritative information in regard to the subject matter covered. It is sold with the understanding that neither the author nor the publisher is engaged in rendering legal, accounting, or other professional service. If legal advice or other expert assistance is required, the services of a competent professional person should be sought.

> —*From a Declaration of Principles Jointly Adopted by a Committee of the American Bar Association and a Committee of Publishers and Associations*

McGraw-Hill books are available at special quantity discounts to use as premiums and sales promotions, or for use in corporate training programs. To contact a representative, please e-mail us at bulksales@mcgraw-hill.com.

This book is printed on acid-free paper.

To my grandparents, **Benjamin Stoken, Ester Kite, Betty Twersky, and Harry Ogens,** who crossed an ocean and settled in an alien culture to provide their descendants the promise of a better life. I hope the book is worthy of you.

Contents

ACKNOWLEDGMENTS

Thanks to:

Larry Bernstein, Kingsley Stoken, and Deidre Stoken McClurg, for patiently reading my manuscript and offering many helpful suggestions. You made it a better book than it would have been.

Joel Weisman, my agent and critic of the first part of the manuscript, for pointing me in the right direction.

Robin Kramer, my faithful assistant, who was always willing and able to perform the numerous chores necessary to bring this project to completion.

Gary Crossland, for providing many of the statistical calculations used in this book.

Michael McClurg, who diligently assisted Deidre with the graphics which enhanced the book.

Finally to the lovely "Sandra Loebe-Stoken," who gets the award for putting up with a mate totally absorbed in his project.

The real trouble with this world of ours is not that it is an unreasonable world, nor even that it is a reasonable one. The commonest kind of trouble is that it is nearly reasonable, but not quite. Life is not an illogicality; yet it is a trap for logicians. It looks just a little bit more mathematical and regular than it is; its exactitude is obvious, but its inexactitude is hidden; its wildness lies in wait.

—G. K. Chesterton

Preface

After graduating from the University of Chicago, School of Business, some 50-years ago, I felt, oh, so smart. I thought I had become a member of a small elite group who really understood our world and had acquired intellectual tools to be successful in whatever I chose to do. In my case, it was to be a trader.

I found an excellent opportunity at the Chicago Mercantile Exchange, where for a nominal sum of money I could purchase a membership and trade directly on the floor. I would be able to use my trading skills to beat the heck out of the market, in that case, a commodities market. Well, it wasn't as easy as I expected. Soon I recognized that all of my previous education was utterly useless in trying to outsmart a "smart" market. I realized that to survive and prosper in the rough-and-tumble environment of a market-place, I would have to unlearn most everything that I had so painstakingly acquired … and discover skills more attuned to dealing with an uncertain future. In this venture, I was completely on my own, as there were no teachers or blueprints to follow.

Bit by bit, by trial and error, as I knew of no other way, I learned how a market worked, with its own peculiar logic—and how to master it. Without realizing it at the time, I had acquired a unique conceptual framework of how the world worked—opening the door to insights into other social areas, such as politics—that was quite different from the Newtonian logical, cause-and-effect construct that had been embedded into my brain from grammar school up through a prestigious graduate university.

I became successful enough so that I was able to retire, at the ripe old age of 31, and self-finance new endeavors. Yet when I tried to communicate what I had learned to others, outside of a few peers at the commodities exchange, I would only elicit glazed eyes or blank stares. You see the language for my new conceptual framework was in my head only, and I lacked a proper vocabulary to articulate it. Even most of my peers were only interested in my conclusions: Is the market headed higher or lower?

In many ways I felt like a lost soul, able only to communicate about mundane things. When talking about more heady matters, I struggled to frame my ideas in a watered-down Newtonian vernacular. It was terribly unsatisfying, as most of the time I was not able to relay to others what I really thought.

Only a few years ago, I discovered the existence of a new science. While browsing a London bookstore I picked up a book, *The Origin of Wealth*, by Eric D. Beinhocker.[1] I started reading it immediately, and my unarticulated ideas bubbled to the surface. I read through the night and into the next. Finally I had found a home for those long-buried notions; I had found a language and an organizational structure through which they could be expressed.

The concept that so tantalized me is called "complex adaptive systems (CAS)": it is a new science that is just now beginning to emerge. Actually, it is more than just a new science. Like the Newtonian "intellectual" revolution, this idea has the potential to become a new mental construct, as Beinhocker states, "the prism through which we conceptually view our universe." CAS, in part a critique on the Newtonian mental construct vigorously publicized by Mr. Beinhocker, is still in its embryonic form. Though the world has not yet taken much notice of the concept, take heed, as it is showing signs of intellectual vigor.

In the mid–1980s, a school in Santa Fe, New Mexico, called the Santa Fe Institute, was founded to study this new science.

New curriculums in complex adaptive systems have already been established at several leading universities, including the University of Michigan, the University of Virginia, and Northwestern University.

In its simplified form, CAS proponents maintain that the Newtonian worldview, which so captivated Western societies after Sir Isaac Newton's seminal discoveries about the motion of heavenly bodies, had hit a brick wall. CAS people readily concede that the Newtonian logical "cause-and-effect" construct played an immense role in propelling Western societies to the forefront of modernity. It enabled us to create precision machinery of all kinds, from trains to planes; it provided a foundation that led to the building of rocket ships capable of taking man to the moon; and it laid the groundwork for our enormous strides in beating back and, in some cases, defeating disease. However, because of that very success we thought it could also be the vehicle to master other areas, such as economics and investing. But in those endeavors, the Newtonian construct has proven to be a dismal failure—one has only to survey the carnage from the financial crisis of the late 2000s that our economic leaders told us *could not* happen. However, repetitive errors didn't stop us. After each blunder we kept thinking we were just one repair job away from mastering those areas, as we had with the hard sciences.

In a nutshell, the Newtonian construct has allowed mankind to acquire a knowledge of linear, cause-and-effect relationships and use them to create mechanical entities, wherein all the interacting parts could be programmed to act in preset ways so that outcomes were highly predictable, for example, airplane accidents are few and far between and the rare mishaps that do occur are identified and fixed so as not to be repeated. As long as the parts to a system are inanimate, this approach works remarkably well. But when the components of a system are humans, as they are in the stock market and the economy, or say a political system, this approach breaks down. This happens because humans are intelligent; they learn, they adapt ... and they cannot be programmed or directed to act in a specific way that will produce a reliable outcome.

Complex adaptive systems built around humans must be approached in a different manner. They are, as their name implies, complex. The large numbers of components that make up the system interact in a non-simple way. There are too many connections to properly understand all of the relationships, which are also continually shifting. And the models the experts build in trying to grasp and analyze these connections are imperfect, and inevitably break down. To understand these systems, we must look for a window to peek inside. And that window is the self-regulating fluctuations, which occur in a trend-like manner.

That is what this book is about: understanding the trends which are the basic mechanisms that underlie stock market movements. In this book, I will teach you how the stock market works and introduce an algorithm, based on these concepts, that has outperformed the stock market on both the return and, even more importantly, the risk side for almost a hundred years.

I will take you on a journey to places conventional financial professionals have not yet visited, to see things you haven't seen before. By the time you emerge at the finish line you will have an entirely different and postmodern way of viewing the stock market—a new investment cosmology. Come with me on this journey.

PART 1

THE ORIGIN OF A NEW INVESTMENT STRATEGY

Investment markets are joined at the hip to our economy, forming a "great wealth-creating system," which we celebrate as free-market capitalism.

We are going to build an investment strategy to exploit our wealth-generating system on principles from evolutionary biology. As we shall see, this robust strategy has proven both more profitable and far less risky than most contemporary stock and bond strategies.

CHAPTER 1

The Investment
Game

Ever since 1792, when a group of stockbrokers, meeting under the now famous buttonwood tree on Wall Street, agreed to form the New York Stock Exchange (NYSE), people have been trying to master the investment game … but with little success.

Sure there have been winners! But in paraphrasing the words of Warren Buffett, head of Berkshire Hathaway and the most quoted investment guru of our time: imagine several million chimpanzees that had been taught to flip a coin, assembled in some immense stadium to participate in a chimp super coin-flipping contest with the media present. As the field narrowed, anxious media members breathlessly interviewed the finalists, asking them, assuming they could speak, what was the basis of their superior coin-flipping skills. And the chimps, honestly believing they possessed some special skill, would credit their success to a particular way of flicking their wrist, or perhaps to repeating some mantra while flipping. The public, meanwhile, listening to the commentator's excited rendition of the chimps' abilities, would believe that practicing such wrist flips or chanting magical mantras led to the chimps' success, and then would try to do the same.

Dear Reader: What if yesterday's and today's acclaimed stock market wizards are no different from a group of chimpanzee finalists?

Sounds silly? Agreed; it flies in the face of the way we Westerners like to think. We are children of a Newtonian mechanistic worldview. More than 300 years ago, Sir Isaac Newton excited our ancestors by solving the problem of the motions of the planets and, in doing so, birthed a new way to look at the world. The Newtonian mechanical worldview championed a chain of cause-and-effect logic and it became the blueprint for a large-scale search for knowledge. As Westerners sought to match cause and effect, identifying a cause for every effect and potential effects of any cause, they created a clear pattern of thinking that allowed us to master problems that had baffled mankind since the ancient Greeks. Over the following centuries, men and women vastly increased our collective store of knowledge; they figured out how to build spaceships that were able to take astronauts to the moon; they invented machines that spearheaded enormous leaps in our world's material wealth; they found cures for numerous diseases that had formerly cut short much of human life; and they designed a system for citizens of a political entity to govern themselves through representatives.

All this is certainly true, yet, whether or not this same type of knowledge can be translated into models that will allow us to reliably predict the future is questionable. Respected observers insist that in the long run the stock market *cannot* be beaten. This means that over time the participants, including so-called experts, will be unable to better an average return obtained from investing in an index of stocks, without taking on a greater amount of risk.

IS THE MARKET BEATABLE?

At the beginning of 1970, there was a haystack of 355 equity funds. We can imagine those funds were run by some of the most savvy and highly paid Wall Streeters, who were backed up by large and highly educated support staffs and enjoyed a huge information advantage over John Q. Public. At the end of 2005, 36 years later, according to John Bogle, founder of the Vanguard Group, 223 of those funds no longer existed. There may be a lot of reasons why funds disappear, but not many of the reasons are good. Of the 132 survivors, only 45—not quite 13 percent—had, even by the tiniest of margins, beaten the Standard & Poor's (S&P) 500. A lonely nine (2.5 percent) achieved that feat by more than a meaningful 2 percent per annum. So an investor's job would be to find those nine needles of outperformers. But wait! Six of the outperformances peaked between 1983 and 1993 and have been struggling ever since. Had you waited more than 7 years to identify those winners, you would have missed most, if not all, of the outperformances. Okay, chimp, go out and find that 1 percent (the three remaining outperformances from the 1970 crop) who are going to be, and remain, winners.

Morningstar, the leading fund statistical rating service, ranks or categorizes funds from one to five stars, with five being the best performing funds. Mark Hulbert, who keeps tabs on real live investment returns, created a hypothetical portfolio that was adjusted to hold only Morningstar's five-star funds. During the 11-year test period, 1994 to 2005, the return was 6.9 percent, which fell way short of an 11 percent total market return during that period. The five-star returns were not even close.

Then there is the story of Bill Miller, star portfolio manager of the Legg Mason Value Trust Fund, who by the early years of the twenty-first century had become an investment legend. By year-end 2005 he had beaten the S&P 500 for 15 straight years. Wow! This was such a statistically improbable event that it was compared to Joe DiMaggio's incredible 56-game hitting streak, a one-in-a-million likelihood. During his streak Miller scored a 15.3 percent compounded return, 2.4 percent better than the S&P 500. It certainly appeared as if we had identified a true investment sage. Magazines, newspapers, and TV commentators fell all over themselves in reporting the "Bill Miller" story and, of course, each of them gave their take on how and why he was such a superior investor. In January 2004, *Money* magazine described Bill Miller as "the country's greatest mutual fund manager." Miller, at that time, had beaten the S&P 500 for 13 years in a row. *Money* computed the odds of doing so at 149,012 to 1. In November 2006, *Fortune* magazine's managing editor, Andy Serwer, seconded Miller's status as "the greatest money manager of our time."

Well what happened? In early 2010, the media's favorite investment "chimp" was replaced as Legg Mason Value Trust Fund's manager. Miller's record, which then included a decline of 55 percent in 2008, was so bad that his Value Trust Fund was ranked by Morningstar close to the bottom for the past 3, 5, and 10 years. The 3-year record was particularly dismal. His fund had an annualized loss of 20 percent, compared to a loss of only 9 percent for the S&P 500. Had you identified "the country's greatest mutual fund manager's" star (!) quality after seven straight S&P 500 beating returns and just prior to the time that Wall Street was beginning to take notice, and invested at the end of 1997, you would have been a net loser when Miller was benched. On the other hand, those investors who ignored Miller's cheerleaders and instead purchased the S&P 500 at the end of 1997 were up approximately 41.5 percent.

CAN WE FORECAST?

Let's now pivot and look at forecasting, which has a lot to do with investing and ask the same question: Can we forecast?

During the 1920s, there was an infectious optimism in the United States. Almost all of the nation's leaders believed there was an enormous pile of new wealth awaiting the middle class— just around the next corner, we were told. In 1929, when the eminent John J. Raskob—chairman of the finance committee of General Motors, vice-president of E. I. DuPont de Nemours & Company, director of Bankers Trust Company, and chairman of the Democratic Party's National Committee—wrote how easy it was to accumulate wealth in a popular article in the *Ladies Home Journal* entitled, "Everybody Ought to B Rich," Americans everywhere nodded their heads in agreement.[1] But when the middle class turned that corner, the goddess of prosperity was nowhere in sight; instead it was the mugger of a depression waiting for them.

In the late 1970s, a baffling inflation had imbedded itself into American economic life; it was turning the nation's financial markets upside down, while a bloated U.S. federal government was encroaching more and more into people's daily lives. To further compound worries, Japan's economy was on the march, crippling such stalwart American industries as autos, steel, and electronics, and threatening to uproot much of the rest of the American economy. Serious Americans plausibly speculated that the nation was in terminal decline and thought the country was headed toward some sort of state socialism. What followed instead was a renaissance of American "free-market" capitalism, just the opposite of what most Americans had been expecting.

Do you remember what the investment world looked like in 1980? The majority of people have long since forgotten, but to refresh memories, the most popular view was one of growing energy shortages and mind-numbing inflation. Howard Ruff and Douglas Casey, the fashionable financial gurus of the time whose best-selling books were being read by millions, were prophesying that the world's supply of oil, the oxygen of industrial economies, was shrinking and oil's price was destined to soon top $100 a barrel; furthermore, inflation, already in double digits was headed into triple digits. The heavy lifters in their recommended portfolios were: gold and silver. As for stocks: Forget it! They were a dead asset, with limited upside potential at best. In fact, a year earlier, *Business Week* magazine, in its cover article, loudly proclaimed, "The Death of Equities."[2] So what happened?

Fast-forward 19 years later, to early 1999:

- Oil was trading at about $11 a barrel, almost 75 percent below its 1980 price and nearly 90 percent beneath its $100 forecasted price.
- Gold was changing hands at $290 an ounce, down about 65 percent from its 19-year earlier price.

- Silver was trading at about $5 an ounce, nearly 90 percent below its 1980 peak price.
- The "dead" asset class equities, the S&P 500, was trading at about 1,275, or up about 1,175 percent from its 1980 low.

These widely accepted forecasts achieved a perfect score; *dead wrong on all four counts.*

Japan's economy continued to thrive throughout the 1980s, in fact, so much so that, almost daily, new books were being published, shouting that Japan's "miracle" economy was about to grind the American and Western economies into the dust. As Clyde Prestowitz, president and founder of the Economic Strategy Institute, wrote in 1988, "Japan has created a kind of automatic wealth machine, perhaps the first since King Midas."[3] However, most authors were kind enough to explain the Japanese economic-business model, which was quite different from the Western model, and urged America to hurriedly adopt Japanese business methods.

How did the highly touted Japanese model do? In early 1999, while world stock markets were trading at more than three times their early-1990 levels, stocks in Japan were trading nearly two-thirds *below* their 1989 year-end prices. In Japan, the 1990s had become the "lost decade." It was a 10-year period of economic stagnation, during which time real estate markets collapsed, bad loans crippled the Japanese banking system, and pension funds began running short of money to pay retirees. To say the least, there was a clear lack of interest in writing or talking about Japanese business savvy by the century's end.

In the mid-1980s, Americans were caught up in a budget deficit mania. Worrywart commentators were talking about a sea of red ink, stretching out as far as the eye could see, that would surely bankrupt the United States ... unless the Reagan tax cuts were reversed. During a 1984 presidential debate, Walter Mondale told cheering Democrats that there had to be a "new realism" in government. "Let's tell the truth," he challenged.

"Mr. Reagan will raise taxes and so will I. He won't tell you. I just did." Reagan won that election and did not raise taxes. In fact, he lowered them … again.

Taxes would not be raised (meaningfully) until the 1990s, and then the upward adjustment would offset only a small portion of the prior Reagan tax cuts. While government debt did quadruple from 1980 until 1992, the American economy did not buckle. Rather, it surged to unprecedented heights, far surpassing Japan's "miracle" economy. And who would have thought that from late 1982 until the end of 2000, a period of 18 years, the nation's economy would experience only one 8-month recession? Never before had an industrial economy experienced such a long run of nearly uninterrupted economic good fortune. As for government deficits as far as the eye could see, well, by the turn of the century, they had become surpluses as far as the eye could see. (The red ink of the early twenty-first century is a new matter—not a direct causality of the Reagan tax cuts.)

Oh yes. let's not forget the widely predicted post–World War II depression. Sewell Avery, head of US Gypsum, had retrenched on the eve of the Great Depression, allowing his company to side-step the troubles that were battering most American businesses. Two years later he was anointed to head Montgomery Ward by John Pierpont (J.P.) Morgan, the largest shareholder of the floundering catalog merchandiser. Avery, the poster boy of inflexibility, hunkered down after World War II, attempting once again to ride out the predicted storm. But there was no depression. Instead the country began a 25-year period of unprecedented prosperity and soaring share prices. And Avery, waiting for hard times that never came, sat on the sidelines while Montgomery Ward shrank to a third-rate company.

These consensus "forecasts" were ALL laughingly wide off the mark. No wonder the late Peter Drucker, who by general consensus had been considered America's foremost business management authority, threw up his hands and said, "Forecasting is not a respectable human activity."

USING NEWTONIAN THOUGHT TO BEAT THE MARKET

So how do we square this "nothing seems to work in trying to best the market" view with our Newtonian mental construct? We don't!

As far as helping to predict market outcomes, the Newtonian "cause-and-effect" logic appears to have been worthless and perhaps even somewhat harmful. Perhaps the best we can do, according to John Bogle, who thinks the market is smarter than us all, is merely mimic the market.

If we hope to have a chance at outdistancing the S&P 500 in total returns, we need a better picture of how markets work. But first, let us pause for a short history lesson of the stock market landscape we are operating in.

CHAPTER 2

THE INVESTMENT ENVIRONMENT: AN EVER-CHANGING LANDSCAPE

The year 1926 was the chosen starting point of a study conducted under the auspices of the University of Chicago—now known as the CRISP database—to tabulate complete equity results, encompassing all stocks. From that date on, stock market data has been considered complete and reliable. It is also the most legitimate marker for a beginning to stock market history.

Today, Morningstar keeps the CRISP flame alive in its annual publication, *Ibbotson 'SBBI' Classic Yearbook*, which updates yearly returns on Stocks (S), Bonds (B), Bills (B), and Inflation (I). Most of the figures we will use in the coming chapters are from the *Ibbotson 'SBBI' Classic Yearbook*. Table 2-1 contains a year-by-year compilation of returns for stocks, intermediate government bonds, and 90-day T-Bills.

To follow the contours of an investment through time, I am going to introduce a new concept for many of you: Net Asset Value (NAV). NAV starts with a hypothetical $1000 and adds or subtracts each subsequent year's performance to the prior year's NAV to derive a total wealth map. Take a look at Table 2-1. In 1926, equities were up 11.62 percent; the original $1000 was multiplied by that percent (1.1162×1000) and added to the original $1000 to get a year-end NAV value of 1116. In the following year, stocks were up another 37.49 percent; this number was used to multiply the prior year's NAV of 1116 and resulted in a 1927 year-end NAV of 1534. A losing year, such as the −8.42 percent

Table 2-1   Stock Market and Intermediate Bond Returns, 1926–2010

YEAR	ALL STOCKS	NAV 1000	POTHOLE PAIN <20%>	INT GOV BONDS	NAV 1000	STKS/BDS 60/40	NAV 1000	POTHOLE PAIN <20%>	90-DAY T-BILLS
1926	+11.62	1116		+5.38	1054	+9.12	1091		+3.27
1927	+37.49	1534		+4.52	1101	+24.30	1356		3.12
1928	+43.61	2203		+0.92	1112	+26.58	1717		3.56
1929	(8.42)	2018		+6.01	1178	(2.65)	1671		4.75
1930	(24.90)	1515		+6.72	1258	(12.25)	1466		2.41
1931	(43.34)	858		(2.32)	1228	(26.93)	1071		1.07
1932	(8.19)	788	(64.21)	+8.81	1337	(−1.39)	1057	(38.44)	0.96
1933	+53.99	1214		+1.83	1361	+33.13	1407		0.30
1934	(1.44)	1196		+9.00	1484	+2.74	1445		0.16
1935	+47.67	1766		+7.01	1588	+31.41	1899		0.17
1936	+33.92	2366		+3.06	1637	+21.58	2309		0.18
1937	(35.03)	1537	(35.03)	+1.56	1662	(20.39)	1838	(20.39)	0.31
1938	+31.12	2015		+6.23	1766	+21.16	2227		(0.02)
1939	(0.41)	2007		+4.52	1845	+1.56	2262		0.02
1940	(9.78)	1810		+2.96	1900	(4.68)	2156		0.00

Table 2-1 Stock Market and Intermediate Bond Returns, 1926–2010 (Continued)

YEAR	ALL STOCKS	NAV	POTHOLE PAIN <20%>	INT GOV BONDS	NAV	STKS/BDS 60/40	NAV	POTHOLE PAIN <20%>	90-DAY T-BILLS
1941	(11.59)	1600	(20.54)	+0.50	1910	(6.75)	2011		0.06
1942	+20.34	1927		+1.94	1947	+12.98	2271		0.27
1943	+25.90	2426		+2.81	2001	+16.66	2649		0.35
1944	+19.75	2905		+1.80	2037	+12.57	2982		0.33
1945	+36.44	3963		+2.22	2083	+22.75	3661		0.33
1946	(8.07)	3643		+1.00	2103	(4.44)	3498		0.35
1947	+5.71	3851		+0.91	2123	+3.79	3631		0.50
1948	+5.50	4063		+1.85	2162	+4.04	3778		0.81
1949	+18.79	4827		+2.32	2212	+12.20	4239		1.10
1950	+31.71	6357		+0.70	2227	+19.31	5057		1.20
1951	+24.02	7884		+0.36	2236	+14.56	5793		1.49
1952	+18.37	9333		+1.63	2272	+11.67	6470		1.66
1953	(0.99)	9240		+3.23	2345	+0.70	6515		1.82
1954	+52.62	14,102		+2.68	2408	+32.64	8641		0.86
1955	+31.56	18,553		(0.65)	2393	+18.68	10,255		1.57
1956	+6.56	19,770		(0.42)	2382	+3.77	10,642		2.46

Table 2-1 Stock Market and Intermediate Bond Returns, 1926–2010 (Continued)

YEAR	ALL STOCKS	NAV	POTHOLE PAIN <20%>	INT GOV BONDS	NAV	STKS/BDS 60/40	NAV	POTHOLE PAIN <20%>	90-DAY T-BILLS
1957	(10.78)	17,639		+7.84	2569	(3.33)	10,288		3.14
1958	+43.36	25,287		(1.29)	2536	+25.50	12,911		1.54
1959	+11.96	28,312		(0.39)	2526	+7.02	13,817		2.95
1960	+0.47	28,445		+11.76	2823	+4.99	14,507		2.66
1961	+26.89	36,093		+1.85	2875	+16.87	16,954		2.13
1962	(8.73)	32,943		+5.56	3075	(3.01)	16,444		2.73
1963	+22.80	40,453		+1.64	3085	+14.34	18,802		3.12
1964	+16.48	47,120		+4.04	3209	+11.50	20,964		3.54
1965	+12.45	52,987		+1.02	3242	+7.88	22,616		3.93
1966	(10.06)	47,657		+4.69	3394	(4.16)	21,675		4.76
1967	+23.98	59,085		+1.01	3428	+14.79	24,881		4.21
1968	+11.06	65,620		+4.54	3584	+8.45	26,983		5.21
1969	(8.50)	60,042		(0.74)	3557	(5.40)	25,526		6.58
1970	+3.86	62,360		+16.86	4157	+9.06	27,839		6.52
1971	+14.30	71,277		+8.72	4520	+12.07	31,199		4.39 All

Table 2-1 Stock Market and Intermediate Bond Returns, 1926–2010 (Continued)

YEAR	ALL STOCKS	NAV	NAV-2 1000	POTHOLE PAIN <20%>	INT GOV BONDS	NAV	STKS/BDS 60/40	NAV	POTHOLE PAIN <20%>	90-DAY T-BILLS
1972	+18.99	84,813	1190		+5.16	4753	+13.46	35,399		3.84
1973	(14.69)	72,379	1015		+4.61	4972	(6.97)	32,931		6.93
1974	(26.47)	53,221	746	(37.5)	+5.69	5255	(13.61)	28,449		8.00
1975	+37.23	73,035	1024		+7.83	5666	+25.47	35,695		5.80
1976	+23.93	90,512	1269		+12.87	6395	+19.51	42,659		5.08
1977	(7.16)	84,313	1179		+1.41	6485	(3.73)	41,068		5.12
1978	+6.57	89,544	1256		+3.49	6712	+6.04	43,548		7.18
1979	+18.61	106,202	1490		+4.09	6986	+12.80	49,123		10.38
1980	+32.50	140,726	1974		+3.91	7259	+21.06	59,468		11.24
1981	(4.92)	133,802	1877		+9.45	7945	+0.83	59,961		14.71
1982	+21.55	162,637	2281		+29.10	10,258	+24.57	74,694		10.54
1983	+22.56	199,323	2796		+7.41	11,018	+16.50	87,018		8.80
1984	+6.27	211,825	2971		+14.02	12,562	+9.37	95,172		9.85
1985	+31.73	279,038	3914		+20.33	15,116	+27.17	121,030		7.72
1986	+18.67	331,134	4344		+15.14	17,405	+16.86	141,436		6.16
1987	+5.25	348,519	4888		+2.90	17,910	+4.31	147,532		5.47

Table 2-1 Stock Market and Intermediate Bond Returns, 1926–2010 (Continued)

YEAR	ALL STOCKS	NAV	NAV-2	POTHOLE PAIN <20%>	INT GOV BONDS	NAV	STKS/BDS 60/40	NAV	POTHOLE PAIN <20%>	90-DAY T-BILLS
1988	+16.61	406,407	5700		+6.10	19,002	+12.41	165,840		6.35
1989	+31.69	535,198	7507		+13.29	21,527	+24.33	206,189		8.37
1990	(3.10)	518,697	7274		+9.73	23,622	+2.03	210,375		7.81
1991	+30.47	676,744	9490		+15.46	27,274	+24.47	261,854		5.60
1992	+7.62	728,312	10,214		+7.19	29,235	+7.45	281,362		3.51
1993	+10.08	801,726	11,243		+11.24	32,521	+10.54	311,017		2.90
1994	+1.32	812,308	11,391		(5.14)	30,849	(1.26)	307,099		3.90
1995	+37.58	1,117,574	15,672		+16.80	36,032	+29.27	396,987		5.60
1996	+22.96	1,374,169	19,271		+2.10	36,789	+14.62	455,026		5.21
1997	+33.36	1,832,592	25,699		+8.38	39,872	+23.37	561,366		5.26
1998	+28.58	2,356,347	33,044		+10.21	43,943	+21.23	680,544		4.86
1999	+21.04	2,852,122	39,997		(1.77)	43,165	+11.92	761,665		4.68
2000	(9.10)	2,592,579	36,357		+12.59	48,599	(0.43)	758,390		5.89
2001	(11.89)	2,284,321	32,034		+7.62	52,302	(4.09)	727,372		3.83
2002	(22.10)	1,779,486	24,955	(37.6)	+12.93	59,065	(8.09)	668,527		1.65
2003	+28.68	2,289,843	32,112		+2.40	60,483	+18.17	789,998		1.02

Table 2-1   Stock Market and Intermediate Bond Returns, 1926–2010 (Continued)

YEAR	ALL STOCKS	NAV	NAV-2	POTHOLE PAIN <20%>	INT GOV BONDS	NAV	STKS/BDS 60/40	NAV	POTHOLE PAIN <20%>	90-DAY T-BILLS
2004	+10.88	2,538,978	35,605		+2.25	61,844	+7.43	848,695		1.20
2005	+4.91	2,663,641	37,354		+1.36	62,685	+3.49	878,315		2.98
2006	+15.79	3,084,230	43,252		+3.14	64,653	+10.73	972,558		4.80
2007	+5.49	3,253,555	45,626		+10.05	71151	+7.31	1,043,652		4.66
2008	(37.00)	2,049,739	28,745	(37.0)	+13.11	80478	(16.96)	866,649		1.60
2009	+26.46	2,592,100	36,350		(2.40)	78,547	+14.92	995,953		0.10
2010	+15.06	2,982,470	41,824		+7.12	84,140	+11.88	1,114,272		0.12

	Equities	Int Gov	SB 60/40	90-Day T-Bill
CMPD Return	+9.87	+5.35	+8.60	+3.62%
Excess Return (Less 3.62)	+6.25	+1.73	+4.98	0
Risk Measures				
Standard Deviation	20.39	5.70	12.41	3.09
Avg. Underperformance	(4.98)	(1.11)	(2.80)	—
Gain to Pain	1.26	1.56	1.78	—
Worst Drawdown	(64.21)	(5.14)	(38.44)	0.02
2nd Worst Drawdown	(37.6)	(2.40)	(20.39)	—
No. Yrs. Outperformed T-Bills	55	53	59	0

in 1929, was used to multiply the prior year's NAV, only this time the figure, which was 185, was subtracted from 1928's NAV of 2203, resulting in a new 1929 NAV of 2018. This annual NAV wealth map allows us to calculate compounded (CMPD) returns or drawdowns (DDs) in equity for any calendar-year interval.

As we can readily see, during the 85-year period ending on December 31, 2010, the stock market, including reinvested dividends, delivered a generous compounded annual return of 9.87 percent. An original $1000 investment at the beginning of 1926 blossomed into $2,982,470 by the period's end. This return was far larger than those from bonds—long-term (20-year) Treasuries returned a paltry compounded 5.5 percent, while the return on intermediate (5-year) government bonds was 5.4 percent (see Table 2-2)—and almost any other asset class that had a sufficiently long enough history to measure.

Table 2-2   Bond Profile, 1926–2010

GOVERNMENT BONDS	CMPD RETURN	ER	AU	G/P RATIO
Long-Term	5.50%	1.88	(2.56)	0.73
Intermediate-Term	5.35%	1.73	(1.11)	1.56

Furthermore, note that these stock market returns beat a riskless 90-day T-Bill in 55 of the 85 years (Table 2-1). That means it paid to take on risk, via equities, approximately 65 percent of the time.

No wonder leading stock market academicians, such as Jeremy Siegel, Professor of Finance at The Wharton School of the University of Pennsylvania and author of the widely read investment classic *Stocks For the Long Run*, stood on soap boxes herding investors into equities only, buy-and-hold (B&H) portfolios with the strict caveat to hang on through thick and thin. But there is another side to the stock market equation …

RISK

Most would answer the risk question by referring you to the standard deviation of stock returns which was 20.39 percent, as shown in Table 2-1. Traditional risk analysis uses *standard deviation*—the variation in annual returns from its average—as a proxy for volatility, which is translated to mean risk. A higher standard deviation means more volatility, and is assumed to imply greater risk and vice versa. Increased volatility certainly does seem to capture certain aspects of risk. Strategies that use more leverage or higher betas (a measure of the volatility of the asset compared to the volatility of the financial market as a whole) are, indeed, likely to display higher standard deviations.

However, standard deviation suffers from assuming investment returns fall into a "normal" distribution pattern, much like in physics or general statistics. But when applied to investing, that normal distribution vastly underestimates tail risk. *Tail risk* refers to outliers on the downside that far exceed what should be normal boundaries to a price decline, such as in 2008 or the one-day stock market plunge of 23 percent in October 1987.

I think we might get a better picture of "risk" by measuring the real recorded S&P 500 average underperformance to a "riskless" 90-day T-Bill, which is the best metric of the actual pain investors suffer, even if only on paper. To do so, we add up all underperforming years and then divide the total by the number of years observed—85 in the present case. This provides an average underperformance (AU) figure for the whole period, which can be an excellent proxy for risk (see Table 2-1). Over the entire 1926–2010 period, equities had an average underperformance of (4.98) percent, with total underperformances of (423.16) divided by 85 observed years. That's pretty steep and probably the very reason some investors keep on walking past the soap boxes without pausing.

An oft-repeated rule in investment circles is that the greater the return, the more the risk—and stock/bond market statistics certainly seem to bear this out. As shown in Table 2-2, long-term 20-year Treasuries had an average underperformance of (2.56), which was 49 percent less than the stock market, over that same 85-year time span. Intermediate (5-year) government bonds were an even safer investment, with a very low average underperformance of just (1.11). Those low average underperformances compensated for the meager compounded returns on the two types of bonds.1

We can take this risk analysis one step further and get a snapshot of the relative risk/reward payoff on different investments. First we subtract the riskless 85-year compounded return on a 90-day T-Bill, which was 3.62 percent, from the compounded gains of each investment. This provides us with the excess return (ER), which is the payoff investors receive for taking on risk. Stocks provided 6.25 percent excess return (a compounded return of 9.87 percent less the 3.62 percent T-Bill return). The excess return for long-term Treasuries was 1.88 percent; intermediate government bonds clocked in at 1.73 percent.

Then we divide the excess return by the average underperformance to arrive at a gain-to-pain ratio, as shown in Table 2-1. The *G/P ratio* is the amount of excess gain each 1 percent of average underperformance, or risk, yields. Equities, with an excess return of 6.25 percent, divided by its AU of (4.98) translates into a G/P ratio of 1.26, which means each 1 percent of risk harvested an excess return of 1.26 percent. Long-term Treasuries, even with a much lower average underperformance, fell way short of that ratio; the payoff for each 1 percent of average underperformance was a mere (0.73). On the other hand, intermediate government bonds provided the most efficient payoff, 1.56 percent of return for each 1 percent of risk. See Table 2-2. Yet, how many investors would be willing to settle for the intermediate government bond's puny 85-year return of $84,140 when a 35-fold greater return of $2.982 million was available, over that same time slot, had they chosen stocks?

Excessive Losses

Another way to look at risk is to view how many times stock market participants suffered excessive losses. We can use 20 percent as the "pain threshold," the equivalent of investor water boarding, because it is the usual definition of a bear market. Peak-to-trough falloffs, including multiple years, of that amount or larger, measured only on the annual calendar year's NAV—disregarding intra year stock market movements—indicate that the stock market has fallen into a deep pothole and it will take a lot of climbing before the stock market reaches its former high watermark. The potholes are highlighted in bold in the pothole pain columns of Table 2-1. During the last 85 years, stocks fell into six potholes (Table 2-3), and they exceeded 20 percent by a combined 111.64 percent. That was 111.64 percent of torture.

Table 2-3   6 Deep Potholes = Loss in Excess of 20%

TOTAL TORTURE YEARS	ALL STOCKS POTHOLES	STKS/BDS 60/40 POTHOLES
1929–1932	(44.21)	(18.44)
1937	(15.03)	(0.39)
1939–1941	(0.54)	—
1973–1974	(17.25)	—
2000–2002	(17.61)	—
2008	(17.00)	—
Total torture	(111.64)	(18.83)

Stock/Bond 60/40

One more thing! In the real world, many investors, especially those who had ignored the soap box orators, are not comfortable with an equity-only strategy. They are more inclined to choose a traditional 60 percent stock/40 percent bond setup (SB 60/40), which has done a fairly good job of reducing risk.

Past history clearly favors the intermediate government bond, which sports a very low (1.11) average underperformance (AU) and a gain-to-pain (G/P) ratio of 1.56 as the preferred fixed-income vehicle, and we will use it (as reported in *Ibbotson*), for the bond portion of our SB 60/40 portfolio (Table 2-1). Investors who substituted intermediate government bonds for 40 percent of their stock investment would have been able to capture a compounded return of 8.60 percent, only 1.27 percent shy of the compounded annual return of 9.87 percent for B&H portfolios, while, and this is important …improving their risk profile dramatically. Average underperformance was cut to (2.80), which was 44 percent below the all-stock portfolio's AU of (4.98). And that provided a gain-to-pain ratio of 1.78, considerably better than B&H portfolio's G/P of 1.26. The SB 60/40 portfolio also beat a riskless 90-day T-Bill portfolio in four additional years than the B&H portfolio did. Furthermore, the SB 60/40 portfolio only fell into two deep potholes, and the total 18.83 percent of torture was much more tolerable than what buy-and-hold investors suffered through.

THE 85-YEAR INVESTMENT LANDSCAPE

This is the map, laying out the contours and potholes, of the past 85-year investment landscape. To summarize:

- Stocks bought and held throughout the last 85 years leading up to 2011 would have produced a compounded return of 9.87 percent …
- … but also an average underperformance of (4.98) to a risk-free investment. By accounting for average underperformance—the underappreciated other side of the risk-to-return equation—market participants may get a clearer picture of what to expect on the risk side

of an investment strategy, something the 1990s and post-2000 stock market participants neglected to do.

- A buy-and-hold investment strategy faced a rough terrain, wherein stocks fell into six deep potholes, each measuring more than 20 percent, inflicting a great deal of pain on participants.
- Including some intermediate government bonds in a portfolio, say about 40 percent, would have allowed investors to navigate that volatile investment landscape with far less pain and only a little less gain.
- Intermediate government bonds have been a good risk-reducing choice for the bond portion of that portfolio, as they came quite close to replicating a riskless 90-day T-Bill, an AU of just (1.11), while allowing an investor to pick up some worthwhile extra return—1.73 percent more than the 90-day T-Bill rate during the past 85 years.

This portrayal of the investment landscape has been, and is, the proper starting point for investors. Until quite recently, it also was the ending point. In fact, it was all you needed to know, as buy and hold became the standard investment strategy. Yes, stock market gurus recommended some diversification into foreign stocks, or the inclusion of small stocks, but those additions hardly moved the result needle.

But is this the best we can do? Perhaps it is, within a Newtonian mechanistic construct. The Newtonian framework of thinking and problem solving, which worked so well in laying a foundation for an industrial world with its enormous economic vitality, has not measured up when applied to areas wherein uncertainty reigns, such as in the economy and in investment markets. The crisis of 2008 was only the last of a long series of crises exposing "how little the experts know" when dealing with uncertainty.

A DARWINIAN FINANCIAL MARKET FRAMEWORK

Investors who hope to outfox the market must first get its conceptual framework right. Systems that operate in spaces wherein uncertainty prevails function by different rules (or laws) than those we are acquainted with. Andrew W. Lo, Professor of Finance at the Massachusetts Institute of Technology, thinks "financial markets are better understood through the lenses of a biologist rather than a physicist."[1] That is, we need to focus on their adaption to changing environments that characterize the biological realm, rather than the sort of immutable laws that form the foundation of physics.

I am going to reach into Darwin's grab bag of biological laws and create three portfolios by combing four of the most important asset classes in our wealth-creating system. The first, geared to conservative investors, is a buy-and-hold portfolio of the four asset classes. The second takes those asset classes active by buying and selling according to a simple algorithm. And because its risk parameters were so benign, I created a third portfolio, which is a leveraged version of the previous one. As we shall see, the performance of all three, on both the return and the risk side, was striking.

But first, in the following two chapters, we will take a look at a different mental construct, a different way of thinking based on Darwinian evolutionary processes.

CHAPTER 3

THE DARWINIAN ALTERNATIVE FRAMEWORK

The recent idea that many of our social entities are "complex adaptive systems (CAS)" has captivated the imaginations of a small but growing group of academics. As this systems theory is still an infant science, there is, as yet, no generally agreed upon definitions of CAS or on precisely how they operate.

In general, these scientists believe there is a limit to how far the so-called Newtonian mental construct can take us. Sure, they acknowledge that Newtonian cause and-effect logic provided a mental model which allowed us to create quite reliable mechanical entities. For example, a watch properly constructed keeps the correct time day after day, year after year, and decade after decade. But the reliability of the model changes when dealing with economies, markets, political systems, and other social entities.

Replace the components of a mechanical system with intelligent humans—call them agents—who think, learn, and adapt, and we have a living social system with a great deal of complexity ... too much so for any individual to gain a proper understanding of the intricate and shifting relationships between the numerous interworking components. Interacting agents (components) have an unlimited degree of freedom to act in unreliable ways, which leads to outcomes that are unpredictable.

Consequently, Newtonians have been unable to shine their bright beam of cause-and-effect logic to illuminate the murky world of human action. Much of the way we think and reason, which works so well in our physical world, breaks down when applied to living systems, leading to an error rate that makes us appear groping in the dark, much like our prehistoric ancestors. However, like humans, complex adaptive systems often display discernible patterns of behavior, and this *may* enable us to make more sense of our social systems.

SELF-ORGANIZATION

Definitions of complex adaptive systems vary, but all characterize them as self-organizing and self-correcting (or self-renewing). That means they operate *without* a director or a central command system. Like a flock of birds taking flight in perfect formation, or cities that spring up out of nowhere, or people walking through Times Square, order spontaneously emerges.

When taking to the air, birds are programmed to instinctively follow a set of simple rules in reacting to their fellow nearby birds. The result is a synchronized flock pattern. Although the situation with humans is more complex, it is not totally dissimilar! People also take cues from those around them, a process that sociologists term "social learning," and this provides for a great deal of synchronization in human activities.

Neuroscientists have shown that we have permeable minds. When we watch somebody do something, we re-create the mental processes in our own brains as if we were performing the action ourselves. Scholars now tell us our so-called rational choice or decision making is powerfully influenced by the social context—the frames, the biases, and the filters that we subconsciously share with others in our social network. In short, the behavior of those around us plays a very important (but generally overlooked) role in instructing us what to do.

In CAS, intelligent agents interact with other agents. Furthermore, they are also responding to a co-evolving outside environment in ways that affect the mental models of the other agents and produce complex patterns of feedback loops, which may either amplify or dampen an effect. The relationships are nonlinear and the emergent outcome, which is more than a sum of the parts, is unpredictable. Small changes sometimes lead to outsized outcomes; take a pile of sand, wherein at some critical point a few additional grains sprinkled on the pile may lead to a small or disproportionally large avalanche; think of the assassination of the Archduke Franz Ferdinand of Austria in Bosnia, which ignited World War I and the death of more than 16 million people. These critical levels are quite important as they indicate an important change in the functioning of the system has taken place.

What we are describing is a vibrant and dynamic capitalist economy. It is also its counterpart, a co-evolving stock market. Both exhibit "spontaneous order" based upon the principle of self-organization and display fluctuations that enable the system to self-correct and build increasingly larger sand piles of networks, which often reach levels wherein a small marginal transaction can set off a downward cascade that ends only after a generation of investors has met up with its financial grim reaper.

The spontaneous order that emerges from an unseen self-organizing property is not unlike that which results from the "invisible hand" described by Adam Smith, the father of classical economics. While complex adaptive systems resemble Smith's "invisible hand," they are not quite the same thing. In Smith's view, an individual "intends only his own gain ... and he is in this ... led by an invisible hand to promote an end which was not part of his intention ... (yet). ... By pursuing his own interest he frequently promotes that of the society more effectually than when he really intends to promote it."

In other words, society benefits by allowing, or even encouraging, people to indulge in their own greed. Economists interpret this to mean that, in a free market, producers seeking profits charge lower prices to undersell competitors or produce higher quality goods, while consumers eager to get the most value for their buck will be discriminating spenders. This results in a price and product distribution most beneficial to the whole society.

A complex adaptive system is Smith's "invisible hand" and more. Add in self-organization, which results from interactions among the agents, information processing, feedback loops, fluctuations to reduce internal pressures, and unpredictable outcomes.

DARWIN'S ALGORITHM: NATURAL SELECTION

While Newtonians derive their legitimacy from the laws of physics, proponents of complex adaptive systems look to Charles Darwin and his theory of evolution, with its own particular logic, for their credibility. These alternative biological laws, which describe the processes that govern the way our social world works, buttress the concept of self-organizing, complex adaptive systems; their logic may be poised for prime time as a supplement to Newtonian logic.

Evolution is simply an algorithm, or formula, which finds designs that improve a species's "fitness" to function within its environment. An enormous number of candidate designs are created, the result of numerous replication imperfections (mistakes), and tried out in the environment. Most, however, are uninteresting, for example, a primitive eyeball that fails to see and does nothing to add to the species' fitness. But a few are what are called "good tricks;" that is, they improve the species' fitness. The problem is how do we find these needles of good tricks in a haystack of uninteresting design changes, and then, if that isn't hard enough, how do we replicate the good ones?

This problem of finding the rare good trick among an overabundance of design mistakes is not unlike our investment problem. It is not easy. If left to human minds, no matter how intelligent, they would probably flub it. But evolution goes about its business through a pragmatic learning process of trial and error, which seeks "good enough" (though not perfect) solutions to problems. Each error, along the way, provides feedback so as to formulate a new trial until a solution is found.

The algorithm operates as an enormously successful search engine, called "natural selection," to find "good tricks" and route them into the gene pool to make for a fitter species. Natural selection works because the possessor of a fitter design has a competitive advantage in attaining the scarce resources that energize life, such as food and water. Every so often, a rare design "good trick," let's say a seeing eyeball, proves to be a fitter trait because it provides its first recipient, let's make it a guy, a significant advantage. He is able to find food faster and more reliably than others. He wins out in the struggle for scarce resources. This means more time and energy are available to find a reproductive partner so as to inject his fitter trait into the gene pool. A replication step kicks in as Mr. "Seeing Eyeball" mates more often, producing more offspring than his contemporaries. Those offspring who inherit his seeing eyeball will also be prolific baby producers. Soon, on a geological clock, seeing eyeball males and females connect and after a while the earth becomes populated with seeing people, who will have replaced blind ancestors. (Naturally, this oversimplified, minimalist description makes no claim to biological sophistication.)

In short, evolution operates via a process of searching through a variety of potential designs, selecting the few that are good enough, and then replicating or amplifying them. Design, selection, and amplification are its three main steps. Although it is a formula filled with errors, it has been successful enough for science to dub a British evolutionary biochemist's statement Orgel's Second Rule, "Evolution is cleverer than you are." There are often hundreds of moving parts to a system. To beat evolution, a human or team of humans has to identify all the important movements and then get their effects right. Lots of luck!

When a good trick is found, it leads to rapid change as the species is redesigned. Once accomplished, nothing much is likely to happen for a long, long while—or until another good trick comes along. Evolutionary biologists call this revolutionary change in the species followed by a long period of stability "punctuated equilibrium." Moreover, you can bet on the fact that further design changes will eventually become necessary. This is because the landscape or environment we are adapting to is also continually evolving and changing, and this will render former competitive edges useless and sometimes even harmful.

THE ALGORITHM OF FREE MARKET–BASED ECONOMIES

The biological laws of nature, which Charles Darwin uncovered, also appear to govern living systems. In fact, contemporary free market–based economies seem to work precisely because they use the same algorithm as evolution. Consider this:

- *The free market operates as an elaborate and hugely successful search engine, using individuals interacting in a market place to sift through a variety of potential designs (businesses) and select those which are "good enough," though not perfect.*
- *Free markets encourage a competitive drive for resources, while keeping outside interference to a minimum.*
- *Free markets allow a basic attribute of human nature, the instinct to copy or mimic success, free play, thereby amplifying (replicating) the selected successes.*
- *Free markets derive their forward momentum via an elaborate set of feedback loops, wherein resources gained by one agent group are passed on to other groups of agents.*
- *Free markets are littered with errors—in fact, an overwhelming number of start-up companies fail—and deal harshly with error makers, stripping them of much, or*

sometimes all, of their financial resources. Errors, as we shall see, play an important and necessary part. Most early inventors, including Thomas Edison and the Wright brothers, were, in fact, tinkerers, eschewing scientific calculations and proceeding via trial and error—with astonishingly high error rates.

- *Free markets fluctuate; they oscillate from up to down and back to up again, and this is quite important. During the exuberant phase of the cycle, errors become embedded into the system and, at some point, interfere with its ability to self-regulate. Reversals are necessary to flush enough of the errors out so that the system can regain its former vitality. Inefficient and outdated businesses must be eliminated. Businesses that had become slothful must trim excess labor, plants, and inventories. A message must be sent to consumers who had been living it up beyond their means to curb their exuberant spending habits and reduce debt. This allows the economy once again to take on a healthy glow, primed for a sound recovery.*

These cyclical fluctuations operate similar to prey/predator models. Imagine two types of animals, let's say, caribou that live off the natural vegetation of the land and their wolf predators. A lot of wolves dining on their prey will deplete the caribou population. But this also will diminish the predator's food supply, and in short order the wolves likewise will begin to die out. Yet before they do, the caribou population, absent large amounts of predators, will recover, and the increased food supply will allow wolves to begin multiplying once more. This system, when out of balance, self-corrects, which prevents it from self-destructing, and so too does the economy and the stock market.

If we dare to interfere with this process, we run the risk of not flushing enough of the errors out of the system. In that case, the correction process can become much longer, and upturns, during that time, are likely to be shorter and more feeble, or unsustainable. This situation actually happened during the Depression, when policies designed to prevent wages from falling, although probably necessary for humanitarian purposes to prevent agent pauperism and potential rebellion, hurt corporate profits and therefore hiring. Unemployment throughout the 1930s stayed above 14 percent.

Then, if we jump across the ocean, there's Japan. In the 1990s and early twenty-first century, Japan served as the poster child for protective government, embedding past errors into the economy.

Free markets also settle into a web of set, fairly stable patterns, which every so often are disrupted by a (little) "big" bang, followed by a period of revolutionary change. Then, just after the agents have adapted to the excessive volatility, the system stabilizes and volatility subsides—"punctuated equilibrium."

These laws of biological evolution provide a very different picture of reality from what we are used to. This world is one of fluctuations, wherein recessions may, in fact, be healthy. A world filled with errors may not be all bad, as they point the way to a new trial, one of which will ultimately provide a solution. Thomas Edison said, "If I find 10,000 ways something won't work, I haven't failed. I am not discouraged because every wrong attempt discarded is just one more step forward."[1] It is a world of both stability (equilibrium) and revolutionary change, and a world made up of complex and difficult-to-understand feedback loops.

Shining a Darwinian Spotlight on Politics

In the Darwinian world of living systems, Newtonian cause-and-effect logic is not likely to get you very far. A case in point comes from the world of politics: To most political pundits, and many Americans on both the left and the right side of the political spectrum, Ralph Nader was the culprit (the cause) responsible for Al Gore's 2000 presidential election defeat. The logical argument went like this: George W. Bush's exceedingly narrow victory was based on a mere 537 Florida votes. Had the "liberal" spoiler, Ralph Nader, not been on the ballot, a majority of his approximately 97,000 Florida votes (presumably mostly from idealistic left-wingers) would have ended up in Al Gore's column and come January 2001, the Democratic party's nominee would have been sitting in the White House.

But not so fast! The idea of Nader as the *cause* for Gore's defeat is much too simplistic. Without Nader in the contest, Gore's campaign strategy, which had been tailored to appeal to the hard-core left, would in all probability have changed. Chances are Gore would have campaigned as more of a Bill Clinton–type centrist. Yet keep in mind, polls from 1999 throughout the primary season consistently showed Gore having trouble winning over the left wing of the Democratic party. While a more centrist message might well have swung more independent votes his way, on the flip side, more of the lefty Democrats (and there were plenty of them), who actually did come back to him in the end, might have sat out the election.

However, as in real life, the situation was even more complicated. The Bush campaign also would have been handled differently. Ralph Nader's candidacy had put the normally Democratic-leaning states of Wisconsin, Washington, Oregon, and Minnesota into play for the Republicans. The Bush campaign, looking for votes, poured money and time into those Nader-friendly states and tilted Bush's message more toward the center. Without the "champion of the left" in the race, those resources would, most likely, have been deployed elsewhere and very well might have produced a treasure lode of additional Bush "Red" state votes and perhaps a significant amount would have been in Florida.

As those unknowns do not lend themselves to precise measurement, it is by no means certain that sans-Nader, Gore would have won! The only certainty is that Nader's entry changed the dynamics of the race. Whether Gore or Bush was the chief beneficiary is debatable. Actually, in response to the out-pouring of blame many Democrats heaped on Ralph Nader for blocking Gore's path to the Oval Office, Al From, Chairman of the Democrat Leadership Council, wrote in the DLC's *Blueprint* magazine, "I think they're wrong. ... The assertion that Nader's marginal vote hurt Gore is not borne out by the polling data. When exit pollsters asked voters how they would have voted in a two-way race, Bush actually won by a point. That's better than he did with Nader in the race."

THE DARWINIAN WORLDVIEW

A Darwinian worldview provides a fresh and clearer lens by which to view reality. It lays the foundation to recognize an underlying, unseen hand, which operates as a governing mechanism in the stock market, along with other social entities. As we might expect, Newtonians are not impressed with the notion of an abstract, difficult-to-measure, unseen hand operating as the governing mechanism for markets and other social entities. Perhaps, in pre-supposing a nonlinear world wherein random disturbances can sometimes lead to unexpected and disproportionate outcomes, it threatens their basic assumptions by implying that trying to link causes to effects is often a futile endeavor.

Then there is that little matter of human fallibility, which Newtonians are on a mission to correct. Yet the laws of evolutionary biology imply that when dealing with complex adaptive systems humans are of necessity immensely fallible.

Nonetheless, modifying our Newtonian construct may be hard to do. You see, you and I were schooled in that worldview, and share its common points of reference. We unquestionably accept it as the foundational underpinning for our understanding of this world. Giving that up for a vocabulary and logic that appears alien to our shared way of thinking means waking up in an unfamiliar world, and feeling much like the scholastics must have felt after Newton came along.

Add in another problem: According to this Darwinian perspective, we (that's you and I) appear to be rather helpless agents at the mercy of these omnipotent systems.

Yes ... but it may also hold out the promise of a new way of thinking about the world and our place within it. Perhaps we may be able to use it to liberate ourselves from the myopia and mood swings, from greed to fear, which constrain most contemporaries, and become "adaptive" agents. That could very well provide (at least until most other agents also adopt it) the edge in the "game" of life.

As we can see, this picture of how evolution works is not all that different from how markets work. Leslie Orgel's second rule is "Evolution is cleverer than you are." Then along came John Bogle, who claimed the market is smarter than us all. So why not simply let "evolution" do the job of outsmarting smart markets?

But before we go into that, we will delve further into two of the ideas from evolutionary biology that have important implications for investors.

CHAPTER 4

THE STOCK MARKET IS
A LIVING SYSTEM

There are two features of living systems that I want to emphasize, as they are quite important and investors should be aware of them.

The first feature is akin to what evolutionary biologists call "punctuated equilibrium," which I introduced in the last chapter. In the early 1970s, scientists Niles Eldredge and Stephen Jay Gould challenged the long-held idea that evolution was smooth and relatively linear. Quite the contrary, they claimed that evolution proceeded in bursts or not at all. They stated that evolution jumps between stability and relative rapidity; long periods of *stasis*, periods wherein the species retain their same form, are interrupted by shorter periods of rapid catastrophic change. They agreed that the long orderly periods of equilibrium (stasis) wherein nothing much happens, evolutionarily speaking, were the more prevalent condition of life. But once the coevolving environment changed, evolution went on a search, a very chaotic and disorderly search, to select one of the many available variations that would improve the species' "fitness" to adapt to the new environment. Thus, long spans of evolutionary equilibrium were punctuated by shorter intense periods of disorder.

AN EVERLASTING CYCLE OF STASIS AND CHAOTIC DISORDER

This movement from order—extended periods of stasis—to chaotic disorder and back again to order appears to be a biological law that also applies to complex living systems. Since the beginning of the Industrial Revolution, our economy has proven remarkably successful at creating and dispersing wealth. We, as agents, have been conditioned by the promise of improved living standards and have come to assume economic growth as the normal and preferred condition of modern life (stasis). The aspiration of the American people to acquire wealth, which is keyed to the economy's growth, has been *the essence of the nation's energy.*

The "economic growth–acquiring wealth" setup, which dominated our history for the past 150 years, plays the stasis role and it is periodically punctuated by "unexpected" crises, such as in 1929, or more recently in 2008. These storms are periods of chaos and disorder, as old familiar relationships are dramatically altered and the very existence of the system is threatened. These periods, in fact, have been associated with the stock market's deep, deep potholes.

Yet what is so surprising to most contemporary observers is the system's miraculous ability to self-repair or regenerate. After a fairly long period of repair, it usually emerges from its near-death experience to begin an even more fabulous period of wealth creation. We, or later generations, then come to see the crisis for what it was—a mere interruption (punctuation) in our orderly economic progression. This "punctuated equilibrium" feature has been prevalent in industrial capitalism since its beginning.

The buy-and-hold, all-stock strategy places its bet on the system's resiliency. It advocates sweating out those deep potholes with a blind Buddhist-like faith in the system's magical ability to regenerate. Up until now the bet has paid off handsomely.

The U.S. economy and stock market have climbed out of each and every one of its deep potholes, and have gone on to reach even higher levels of economic achievement, rewarding long-term investors with ever greater profits. Nonetheless, B&H investors may be following a flawed strategy. And that brings us to a second important feature of a living system.

NOTHING LASTS!

Living systems, like all biological life, do not last indefinitely! They emerge, grow, reach a moment of glory, and then they begin what is usually a long, slow decline, before finally becoming extinct—or mutating. They are part of a Darwinian world, wherein *nothing lasts*.

Some living systems reach a pinnacle of wealth and power, making them the envy of their region or perhaps even the world. They seem invincible. Historical examples include the Roman Empire, the colossus of the Ancient World; France of the Louis XVI era, with its rank and privileged aristocracy; and the antebellum American South, with its large, slave-holding plantations.

Some historians speculate that these types of entities emerge with a muscular and energetic culture, stressing Spartan-like discipline that bends the agents to sublimate their physical appetites and sacrifice for the sake of the system. With the belief the system is working for them, they flock to the colors and are quite willing to endure enormous hardship to ensure the system's viability. This enables the entity to soak up new energy—most important for an economy is attracting new agents, which leads directly to enlarged markets and new innovational possibilities— and flourish, beating out other rival systems, to survive for many generations. If the entity is truly "adaptive," survival may be stretched to hundreds of years.

Eventually the system's continued successes appear more assured, and its culture evolves into one that is more agent-friendly. A hardworking and purposeful agent population, which had thrived on challenging work, or battle, softens and gives in to its physical appetites, usually little by little. After a while, the leaders and their supporting cast come to feel entitled, and this inevitably leads to a culture that tolerates self-indulgence, decadence, favoritism, and corruption. The agents, without the benefit of the iron-clad discipline of their forefathers, become increasingly unable or unwilling to meet difficult challenges and the system approaches the long slippery slope of decline and fall. It becomes more difficult for the system to attract new energy (new recruits or surges of liquidity to empower agents) and puts it on a one-way track that leads directly into the dustbin of history.

The end may be harsh and bloody, such as the sacking and plundering of Rome by the Visigoths and then by the Vandals, the Jacobin mob-inspired guillotining of the French aristocracy, or the burning and plundering of everything in its puts it as General Sherman's Union army marched through the belly of the Deep South.

Of course, not all systems face such cruel and violent endings. Nonetheless, there is always a system grim reaper lurking in the shadows. And it is quite unlikely that our free-market economy, with its attached stock market, will escape this biological fate.

To be sure, our grand "wealth-generating economic system" appears to still have a great deal of potential new energy sources, as the poor in China, India, Latin America, and other underdeveloped nations have yet to be absorbed into the global economy, and that can be an enormous system driver for generations to come. However, on the flip side of the coin, the muscular agent culture, one of the most important attributes contributing to the virulence of the system, seems to be on the decline in the West. Because of this aspect, there is a great deal of speculation that while the system is still viable, the more muscular and disciplined Eastern nations will soon take the reins. Perhaps!

Obviously, the rise and fall of nations and civilizations is considerably more complex than described here (a host of other factors, some known and some not, are ignored), but they do not change the main Darwinian point—Nothing lasts! Also, I'm aware this idea is not a particularly appealing one, but the reason you are reading this book is to try deal with it.

Keep in mind, most agents in a system are totally attached to their system (albeit with some usually small, out of sync, alienated substratum). They are believers. Their aspirations are in tune with the system's promises, and they are thoroughly conditioned to play their parts as perpetrators of the system. They are, more or less, oblivious to the idea of the system's limited existence. And if, perchance, the idea of extinction was to gain too great a following, agents would not be so willing to play their difficult and often punishing parts, and undoubtedly this would hasten the decline and fall of the system.

Actually there is no actuarial age of extinction for living social systems that we know of. Surely, systems may carry on for quite a while after the agent culture softens; while on the other hand, they can also lose their resiliency and fade away long before the well of new human energy runs dry. We shall see—or rather our grandkids may.

THE RISK OF RUIN

As we cannot be sure of where on its biological time clock our "wealth-generating" system is—infancy, youth, maturity, or old age—there is a particular difficulty in dealing with extreme threats. That is, we cannot be so certain of its resiliency. We cannot know, for sure, that some serious crisis will *not* lead all the way to extinction (or mutation). Nor can we be sure that this system will produce the same results during maturity as it did in its youthful and vigorous growth phase.

Once extinction enters into the equation, we encounter an entirely different type of risk—the "risk of ruin" (in this case, financial extinction). It is qualitatively different from ordinary risk, which can be mathematically calculated and measured by its relation to potential reward. When survival is at stake there is no formula for how much of one's resources should be put at risk. The answer is very little—if any. Most must be redirected to the battle for survival.

Buy-and-hold stock market investors playing out their "sit-on-their-hands" script, are, unbeknownst to themselves, taking on this enormous risk of ruin. They are playing the financial equivalent of Russian roulette, with a bullet lodged in one of the multiple crisis chambers. So far each serious crisis has produced the mere click of an empty chamber. And though there are probably still more empty chambers, we should keep in mind that there is also a bullet, with our name written on it, lodged in one of those remaining chambers. To drive home this extinction point, investors should be aware of the fact that during the last 100 years, military and political upheaval left more than a few stock exchanges defunct or at least moribund for long periods of time. Early in World War I, the stock exchange in St. Petersburg, Russia, shut down; this shutdown lasted for about 75 years. Following the communist takeover of China in 1949, the Shanghai stock exchange suspended operations for over 40 years. Other financial exchanges— including ones in Cairo, Bombay, and Buenos Aires—suffered similar fates.

There is also another popular strategy, although not much, if any, forethought is given to it. It is usually implemented on the spot by investors who don't have a defensive strategy. We know it as "panicking," whereby investors sell the bulk of their investments, most likely near the very bottom of some deep pothole, and retreat into survival mode to protect what's left of their financial resources so they can fight another day. Obviously, over the past 200 years or so, this strategy has been belittled, as it has not served its practitioners very well. Nonetheless, by conserving a good deal of one's remaining financial resources it may, in fact, be a more correct crisis strategy. That is because buy-and-hold investors are risking everything, and at some point in time they, or their grandchildren's grandchildren, may well lose all they have. This will leave them without booty for the world that emerges in the wake of the old system.

To sum up: During a serious crisis, there are usually two main strategies for investors to choose from. One is to pull the trigger and hope the bullet isn't lodged in that chamber; the other is to wave good-bye to a huge chunk of their stash. When faced with two very unappealing choices, the amateur philosopher, Woody Allen, who masquerades as a comic, offered up a strategy. He warned, "More than any time in history, mankind faces a crossroads. One path leads to despair and utter hopelessness, the other to total extinction." His strategy, "Let us pray that we have the wisdom to choose correctly."

Neither strategy is very appealing. And for us, unlike Woody Allen, turning it into a laughing matter is not a viable option.

In Chapters 5 and 6, we introduce another passive (buy-and-hold) strategy, designed around the Darwinian concept of variation, to dramatically reduce risk and provide investors with a much better chance to dodge that bullet and survive in an ever-changing investment landscape.

PART 2

VARIATION: THE FIRST IMPORTANT DARWINIAN INSIGHT

Variation plays an important role in evolution because it allows for alternative designs (traits), some of which likely provide the species with a better "fit" to a changing environment. Successful investing also requires design (asset class) "variation." When equities are not well suited to the prevailing investment climate, an alternative asset class may, by providing a better "fit," save the day.

I am going to introduce three additional asset classes and combine them with the S&P 500 in a buy-and-hold portfolio. This portfolio, consisting of four asset classes, has proven considerably less risky than a stand-alone S&P 500 buy-and-hold strategy, and has actually provided investors with a larger return to boot.

CHAPTER 5

AN ALTERNATIVE INVESTMENT PORTFOLIO: BASED ON VARIATION

The stock market has served to channel a good portion of the generous profits that productive businesses earn into investors' pockets via dividends and capital gains. Given those handsome returns, stocks have won out, hands down, as the "fittest" investment asset class available to investors. According to leading stock market authority, Professor Jeremy Siegel, "The stock market is the driving force behind the allocation of the world's capital. Stocks hold the key to enriching the lives of all peoples everywhere."[1] Siegel, in his book, advocated that investors with time horizons of 30 years or more maintain portfolios consisting of equities only. He thought equities, if kept for that time period, were basically "riskless." According to his research, stocks had always produced a positive return and outperformed bonds to boot over each 30-year period. This sounds good, but such an "all eggs in one basket" approach ignores both the "risk of ruin" and the important role that "variation" plays in both evolution and social systems.

Evolution works because the enormous amount of variation in a species gene pool permits evolution's algorithm to search out "fitter" traits, a few of which will enable the species to adapt to changes in the external landscape. Sufficient variation can also play a key role in creating an effective investment strategy, though not just any variation. The diversity required consists of *alternative* asset classes that are related to *different* components within our "wealth-generating system" and are also *negatively correlated* to equities and to each other.

When our wealth-generating system is working properly, savings and other forms of capital flow abundantly into productive enterprises, and this component generates enormous wealth, becoming the engine that is driving system growth. But this component is only one within this system. There are other important components in our "wealth-generating system," such as a financial subsystem and a huge property market; at times they suck up large portions of the capital and savings that would ordinarily be deployed in productive business ventures.

OUR FINANCIAL SYSTEM

Our financial system is composed of money and credit. Dollars and cents lubricate the exchange process for goods and services and also provide a handy way to convert excess earnings—both wages and profits—after spending, into savings, which can then be rechanneled back into investments, reenergizing the system. In fact, without money, a highly complex economy such as ours would probably not be able to function.

Yet money is an imperfect tool. Its value, much like share prices of business corporations, is in constant flux, going up and down in relation to what it can buy. Rising prices signal *inflation*, which means that the value of money is falling in relation to the goods it can purchase. On the flip side, falling prices signal *deflation*, which means that the value of money is increasing; each dollar can buy more goods and services than it was able to last year, or sometimes even last month. And, oh yes, in our juiced up (credit-fueled) economy, there is also *disinflation*, which means inflation, though present, is moderating or decreasing; this condition is somewhat similar to deflation.

Let's pause here to survey the U.S. price history since 1913, the year the government began publishing the consumer price index (CPI).

The consumer price index, presumed to reflect the price of a basket of goods necessary to maintain the lifestyle of an average family, is compiled on a monthly basis. Table 5-1 shows the actual year-end CPI index price, along with its rate of change from the prior year.

Table 5-1   CPI: History of the Price of Money, 1913–2010

	YEAR-END		RATES OF CHANGES	
YEAR	CPI	ANNUAL %	3-YR. COMPOUNDED %	10-YR. TREND
1912	9.8*			
1913	10.0	2.0		
1914	10.1	1.0		
1915	10.3	2.0	1.7	
1916	11.6	12.6	5.1	
1917	13.7	18.1	*10.7*	Up (*estimated*)
1918	16.5	20.4	17.0	
1919	18.9	14.6	***17.7***	**PEAK**
1920	19.4	2.7	12.3	
1921	17.3	(10.8)	1.6	
1922	16.9	(2.3)	*(3.6)*	Down (*estimated*)
1923	17.3	2.4	(3.7)	
1924	17.3	0.0	0.1	
1925	17.9	3.5	2.0	
1926	17.7	(1.5)	0.6	
1927	17.3	(2.1)	(0.1)	
1928	17.1	(1.0)	(1.5)	
1929	17.2	0.2	(1.0)	
1930	16.1	(6.0)	(2.3)	
1931	14.6	(9.5)	(5.2)	
1932	13.1	(10.3)	***(8.6)***	**TROUGH**
1933	13.2	0.5	(6.6)	
1934	13.4	2.0	(2.7)	
1935	13.8	3.0	1.8	

Table 5-1   CPI: History of the Price of Money, 1913–2010 *(Continued)*

| YEAR | YEAR-END | | RATES OF CHANGES | |
	CPI	ANNUAL %	3-YR. COMPOUNDED %	10-YR. TREND
1936	14.0	1.2	2.1	Up
1937	14.4	3.1	2.4	
1938	14.0	(2.8)	0.5	
1939	14.0	(0.5)	(0.1)	
1940	14.1	1.0	(0.8)	
1941	15.5	9.7	3.3	
1942	16.9	9.3	6.6	
1943	17.4	3.2	7.3	
1944	17.8	2.1	4.8	
1945	18.2	2.2	2.5	
1946	21.5	18.2	7.3	
1947	23.4	9.0	9.6	
1948	24.1	2.7	*9.8*	**PEAK**
1949	23.6	(1.8)	3.2	
1950	25.0	5.8	2.2	
1951	26.5	5.9	3.2	
1952	26.7	0.9	4.2	
1953	26.9	0.6	2.4	
1954	26.7	(0.5)	0.3	Down
1955	26.8	0.4	*0.2*	**TROUGH**
1956	27.6	2.9	0.9	
1957	28.4	3.0	2.1	
1958	28.9	1.8	2.5	
1959	29.4	1.5	2.1	
1960	29.8	1.5	1.6	
1961	30.0	0.7	1.2	
1962	30.4	1.2	1.1	
1963	30.9	1.6	1.2	
1964	31.2	1.2	1.4	
1965	31.8	1.9	1.6	

Table 5-1   CPI: History of the Price of Money, 1913–2010 (Continued)

| YEAR | YEAR-END | | RATES OF CHANGES | |
	CPI	ANNUAL %	3-YR. COMPOUNDED %	10-YR. TREND
1966	32.9	3.3	2.2	
1967	33.9	3.0	2.8	Up
1968	35.5	4.7	3.7	
1969	37.7	6.1	4.6	
1970	39.8	5.5	5.4	
1971	41.1	3.4	5.0	
1972	42.5	3.4	4.1	
1973	46.2	8.8	5.2	
1974	51.9	12.2	8.1	
1975	55.5	7.0	9.3	
1976	58.2	4.8	8.0	
1977	62.1	6.8	6.2	
1978	67.7	9.0	6.9	
1979	76.6	13.3	9.7	
1980	86.3	12.4	*11.6*	**PEAK**
1981	94.0	8.9	11.5	
1982	97.6	3.9	8.3	
1983	101.3	3.8	5.5	
1984	105.3	3.9	*3.9*	Down
1985	109.3	3.8	3.8	
1986	110.5	1.1	2.9	
1987	115.4	4.4	3.1	
1988	120.5	4.4	3.3	
1989	126.1	4.6	4.5	
1990	133.8	6.1	5.1	
1991	137.9	3.1	4.6	
1992	141.9	2.9	4.0	
1993	145.8	2.8	2.9	
1994	149.7	2.7	2.8	
1995	153.5	2.5	2.7	

Table 5-1   CPI: History of the Price of Money, 1913–2010 *(Continued)*

	YEAR-END		RATES OF CHANGES	
YEAR	CPI	ANNUAL %	3-YR. COMPOUNDED %	10-YR. TREND
1996	158.6	3.3	2.8	
1997	161.3	1.7	2.5	
1998	163.9	1.6	2.2	
1999	168.3	2.7	2.0	
2000	174.0	3.4	2.6	
2001	176.7	1.6	2.5	
2002	180.9	2.4	2.4	
2003	184.3	1.9	*1.9*	**TROUGH**
2004	190.3	3.3	2.5	
2005	196.8	3.4	2.8	
2006	201.8	2.5	*3.1*	Up
2007	210.0	4.1	*3.3*	**PEAK**
2008	210.2	0.1	2.2	
2009	215.9	2.7	2.3	
2010	219.2	1.5	*1.4*	Down

1982–1984 = 100
* = beginning of 1913
CMPD rate 1912–2010 = 3.0

To make some sense out of this long series of numbers, I toned down the year-to-year noise by adding in the third column a 3-year compounded rate of price increase (or decrease as the case may be), which smoothes results. This rate also enables us to identify long-term trends in the tempo of prices. A rise or fall in the 3-year rate above or below a decade's long trend (10 years) of prior 3-year rates is normally a sufficient period of time to corroborate that an important change in the trend of prices is under way. (Naturally, we will not be alerted to these trend shifts until well after the direction of prices has actually changed, but that is not important for our purposes.)

Now identifying prior peaks and valleys in the rate of inflation becomes easy. Following a 10-year turn up in the 3-year rate, the highest 3-year rate from then on until the 10-year trend turns down marks an important peak in the rate of inflation. For example, the 10-year trend on the 3-year rate turned up in 1967, and that rate continued to make higher highs until it reached 11.6 percent in 1980. When it subsequently made a 10-year low in 1984, we were able to validate the 1980 number as the "peak" rate. On the flip side, following a turndown in the 10-year trend, the lowest 3-year rate until the 10-year trend turns up is the "trough" rate. This low rate would be the 1.9 percent 3-year rate in 2003 following the 1984 downtrend. It was confirmed as the trough rate when the 10-year trend turned up in 2006.

By focusing on these 3-year peaks and troughs, we get a 98-year map of the changing value of money. We can now readily see that the value of money is rarely stable for very long (see Figure 5-1).

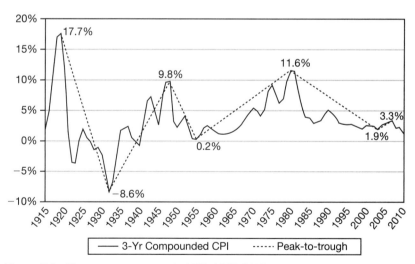

Figure 5-1   Three-year compounded CPI, 1915–2010.

The 3-year compounded rate of inflation reached a peak of 17.7 percent in 1919, fell to a deflationary (8.6) percent in 1932, and by 1948 was, once again, back up to 9.8 percent. From that point, the 3-year rate receded to 0.2 percent in 1955 and then began a long trek of ever-rising inflation that peaked in 1980 at 11.6 percent. A long period of moderating inflation followed and didn't reach its nadir until the 3-year rate had fallen to 1.9 percent in 2003. It was followed by a brief turn up in inflation, which peaked at 3.3 percent in 2007, and then turned down once more at the end of 2010, registering 1.4 percent.

All in all, we can detect four long-term trends of rising inflation separated by three long downtrends in the rate of price increase. See Table 5-2.

Table 5-2   Long-Term Trends in Inflation /Deflation and Their Impact on Gold, Treasuries, REITs, and Equities

CPI IN:

UPTREND = RISING PRICES

	GOLD	TREASURIES		STOCKS	REITs
		LONG-TERM	INTERMEDIATE		
1912–1919	+2.0*	†	+3.4	‡	
1933–1948	+3.7	+3.0	+10.8		
(1956–1971)**	+2.0	+4.1	+8.8		
(1972–1980)**	+33.3	+2.9	+5.4	+7.8	+12.5
2004–2007	+19.1	+6.8	+4.1	+9.2	+13.9

DOWNTREND = FALLING PRICES

	GOLD	TREASURIES		STOCKS	REITs
		LONG-TERM	INTERMEDIATE		
1920–1932	+6.0*	†	+ 3.7‡		
1949–1955	+ 1.8	+ 1.5	+24.2		
1981–2003	(1.5)	+11.4	+9.7	+12.9	+13.1
2008–2010	+19.3	+ 5.7	+5.7	(2.9)	+ 0.7

*1912–19 and 1920–25 portion of first downtrend estimated based on Sidney Homer's *A History of Interest Rates*, published by Rutgers State University in 1963.

† Before 1926, intermediate government bond statistics unavailable.

‡ Pre-1926 figures were also taken from *Ibbotson 'SBBI' Classic Yearbook*, but from a section that was acknowledged to be of lower quality and presumably not a complete list of all NYSE stocks.

** 1956–1980 period broken into two parts as gold and REIT statistics were not available until 1972.

Not too long after prices begin rising, inflation starts heating up and capital flows become diverted into the byways and back alleys of the investment world. Historically, the primary investment back alley has been gold. As we can see from Table 5-2, gold has done an excellent job of shadowing the uptrends in the general price level—a 33 percent compounded return during the 1972–1980 period and a 19.1 percent compounded return from 2004 to 2007. Gold also performed remarkably well—a 19.3 percent compounded return—during the 2008–2010 disinflationary period, wherein excessive government debt appeared to have shaken faith in the paper dollar.

A BIT OF GOLD HISTORY

During most of the nineteenth century, and up until the Great Depression of the 1930s, the price of gold was fixed at $20.67 for a troy ounce. In 1934, during the Great Depression, President Franklin Delano Roosevelt boosted its price to $35, but prohibited American citizens from owning the yellow metal (although gold jewelry and coins were still permitted). Ten years later, at a monetary conference held at Bretton Woods, New Hampshire, the U.S. dollar's link to gold at $35 an ounce was formalized, and the dollar with its gold link became the anchor currency to a new system of fixed exchange rates. As quotes remained at or wobbled on either side of that official price, gold was a dead asset until August 1971, when President Richard Nixon ended the Bretton Woods fixed exchange rate accord and broke gold's link to the U.S. dollar. Soon after, gold became a live asset. Gold was now free to seek a market price and begin trading freely in several market-places, including Switzerland, Singapore, and Canada. U.S. citizens, however, had to wait until December 31, 1974, to own gold outright. We will begin our gold trading history at the end of 1971, just after gold became a live asset. (Gold returns are presented later in Table 5-5.)

Twice a day, in the AM and PM, following a telephone meeting of representatives from five of the larger firms on the London

Bullion Market, a gold quote is posted, and called "the fix." The PM fix has been considered the benchmark of all international pricing since 1919, and we will use it as our gold price in the remainder of this book.

LONG-TERM TREASURIES

On the flip side of the coin, when the price level is falling, bonds tend to be quite a good investment. Fears of inflation are put to rest and investors become more attracted to debt instruments, especially when they see signs of economic turbulence on the horizon. In that case, money that might have gone into the stock market is redirected into bonds, which has the allure of more predictable returns.

I am going to pivot at this point from the intermediate-term government bond (5-year maturity) to the long-term Treasury (20-year maturity) because its longer duration makes it more sensitive to changes in the rate of inflation, thus providing more bang for the buck when inflation is falling, although when prices are heating up, the opposite is likely to occur. The net result, though, is that the 20-year Treasury has a decidedly greater negative correlation, both to the S&P 500 and to the other alternative assets, and that, as we will see later, is a plus for a portfolio designed to minimize risk (see Tables 5-3 and 5-4). Also, during the last two downdrafts in the rate of inflation (1949 to 1955 and 1981–2003) compounded returns for long-term Treasuries of 1.8 percent and 11.4 percent compared favorably to the returns of intermediate government bonds—1.5 percent and 9.7 percent.

If we look at Table 5-2 once again, we see long-term Treasuries did pretty well during downtrends in the rate of inflation, although the correlation is not quite so clear cut as in the case of gold. Long-term Treasuries clearly did nicely during the 1981–2003 period of moderating inflation, almost equaling the return on equities. Long-term Treasuries also did well enough to beat stocks during the 1919–32 period. But, as we can see, during the

Table 5-3   Negative Correlation to the S&P 500 (1972–2010)

	NC*	TY†	NC/TY RATIO
1. Gold	18	39	46%
2. Long-Term Treasuries	15	39	38
3. Intermediate Treasuries	12	39	31
4. REITs	9	39	23
5. AIP	9	39	23
6. Russell 2000‡	6	32	19
7. EEM**	4	23	17
8. Nasdaq	4	39	10
9. MSCI††	3	39	8

* Negative correlation.
† Total years.
‡ Russell 2000 Index began in 1979.
** EMM (Morgan Stanley Index of Emerging Markets) began in 1988.
†† Morgan Stanley Capital International Index of Developed Stock Markets.

Table 5-4   Negative Correlation of Each of the Three Alternative Asset Classes to Each Other

	NC*	TY†	NC/TY RATIO
1. Gold	40	78	51%
2. Long-Term Treasuries	33	78	42
3. REITs	31	78	40
4. Intermediate Treasuries	25	78	32

* Negative correlation.
† Total years.

1949–55 price downtrend, the performance of long-term Treasuries was strictly mediocre. Probably the fact that, unlike at peak inflation rates in 1920 and 1981, the 1949–55 period began with the long-term rate at approximately 2.5 percent, which was quite close to its all-time low yield (not much rate downside left) and which proved too much of a handicap to overcome. (*Ibbotson* reports annual returns on long-term Treasuries. Those returns since 1972 are recorded in Table 5-5.)

Table 5-5 Alternative Investment Portfolio, 1972–2010; Gold, Long-Term Treasuries, and REITs

YEAR	Gold			LT-Treasuries		REITs		
	PRICE*	RETURNS	NAV 1000	RETURNS	NAV 1000	INDEX	RETURNS	NAV 1000
1971	$43.625					100.00		
1972	$64.90	48.75%	1487	5.69%	1057	108.01	8.01	1080
1973	112.25	72.96	2573	(1.11)	1045	91.25	(15.52)	913
1974	186.50	66.15	4275	4.35	1091	71.72	(21.40)	717
1975	140.25	(24.80)	3215	9.20	1191	85.56	19.30	856
1976	134.50	(4.10)	3083	16.75	1390	126.28	47.59	1263
1977	164.95	22.64	3781	(0.69)	1381	154.59	22.42	1546
1978	226.00	37.01	5180	(1.18)	1365	170.57	10.34	1706
1979	522.80	131.33	11,983	(1.23)	1348	231.73	35.86	2317
1980	589.50	12.76	13,511	(3.95)	1295	288.20	24.37	2882
1981	397.50	(32.57)	9111	1.86	1319	305.50	6.00	3055
1982	456.90	14.94	10,472	40.36	1851	371.49	21.60	3715
1983	382.40	(16.31)	8765	0.65	1863	485.30	30.64	4853
1984	308.30	(19.38)	7066	15.48	2151	586.86	20.93	5869
1985	326.80	6.00	7490	30.97	2817	698.93	19.10	6989

Table 5-5 Alternative Investment Portfolio, 1972–2010: Gold, Long-Term Treasuries, and REITs (Continued)

YEAR	Gold			LT-Treasuries			REITs		
	PRICE*	RETURNS	NAV	RETURNS	NAV	INDEX	RETURNS	NAV	
1986	388.80	18.97	8911	24.53	3509	832.83	19.16	8328
1987	484.10	24.51	11,096	(2.71)	3414	802.51	(3.64)	8025
1988	410.30	(15.24)	9404	9.67	3744	910.74	13.49	9107
1989	398.60	(2.85)	9136	18.11	4422	991.26	8.92	9920
1990	386.20	(3.11)	8852	6.18	4695	839.09	(15.41)	8391
1991	353.15	(8.56)	8094	19.30	5601	1138.61	35.70	11,386
1992	332.90	(5.73)	7630	8.05	6052	1304.73	14.59	13,047
1993	386.10	15.98	8849	18.24	7156	1561.17	19.65	15,612
1994	383.25	(0.74)	8784	(7.77)	6600	1610.67	3.17	16,107
1995	387.00	0.98	8870	31.67	8690	1856.57	15.27	18,566
1996	369.25	(4.59)	8463	(0.93)	8609	2511.32	35.27	25,113
1997	290.20	(21.41)	6651	15.85	9973	3020.11	20.26	30,201
1998	287.80	(0.83)	6596	13.06	11,276	2491.53	(17.50)	24,915
1999	290.90	1.08	6667	(8.96)	10,266	2376.42	(4.62)	23,764
2000	274.45	(5.65)	6290	21.48	12,471	3002.97	26.37	30,030

Table 5-5 Alternative Investment Portfolio, 1972–2010: Gold, Long-Term Treasuries, and REITs (Continued)

YEAR	Gold			LT-Treasuries			REITs		
	PRICE*	RETURNS	NAV	RETURNS	NAV	INDEX	RETURNS	NAV	
2001	276.50	0.75	6337	3.70	12,932	3421.37	13.93	34,214
2002	347.20	25.57	7958	17.84	15,239	3552.10	3.82	35,521
2003	416.25	19.89	9540	1.45	15,460	4871.12	37.13	48,711
2004	435.60	4.65	9984	8.51	16,776	6409.30	31.58	64,093
2005	513.00	17.77	11,758	7.81	18,086	7188.85	12.16	71,888
2006	632.00	23.20	14,485	1.19	18,301	9709.31	35.06	97,093
2007	836.50	32.36	19,173	9.88	20,109	8185.75	(15.69)	81,857
2008	865.00	3.41	19,825	25.87	25312	5097.46	(37.73)	50,974
2009	1104.00	27.63	25,304	(14.90)	21,540	6524.25	27.99	65,243
2010	1421.10	28.72	32,571	10.14	23,724	8347.58	27.95	83,478

Table 5-5   Alternative Investment Portfolio, 1972–2010; Gold, Long-Term Treasuries, and REITs (Continued)

	GOLD	LONG-TERM TREASURIES	REITS	S&P 500*
CMPD Return	9.34	8.46	12.01	10.05
T-Bill	5.56	5.56	5.56	5.56
Excess Return	3.78	2.90	6.45	4.49
Standard Deviation	30.09	12.00	18.94	18.33
Avg.Underperf.	(7.18)	(3.43)	(4.74)	(5.10)
G/P Ratio	0.53	0.85	1.36	0.88
Worst Drawdown	(53.41)	(14.90)	(47.50)	(37.61)
2nd Worst Drawdown	(27.88)	(8.96)	(33.61)	(37.31)
No. of Yrs.				
Outperform T-Bill.	20	23	29	26

*PM Fix 12/31 of the stated.

† See Table 5-6.

As we can see, gold and long-term Treasuries have done a pretty good job of allowing investors to take advantage of the secular fluctuations in the rate of inflation (or deflation). Gold is the asset class to hold when inflation is trending higher; long-term Treasuries are the preferred investment when the price level is on a downward slope. Together they provide an alternative opportunity for investors to generate wealth when the financial system is playing havoc with equities, or conversely, a way to benefit when stock market problems are unsettling the financial system.

A Gold/Long-Term Treasury Portfolio

Although both gold and long-term Treasuries had 39-year compounded returns that trailed the S&P 500 by 0.71 percent and 1.59 percent, respectively, when traded together as a portfolio. The two combined held up quite well compared to the S&P 500's results, as shown in Table 5-6. Its 9.96 percent compounded return was only a tad shy of a buy-and-hold portfolio. But more tantalizing was its average underperformance, which, at (3.39), came in approximately 34 percent lower than the S&P 500 number. The result was a gain-to-pain ratio of 1.30, which was actually about 48 percent better than S&P 500's gain-to-pain ratio of 0.88 for the 1972–2010 period.

Table 5-6   AIP versus S&P 500, 1972–2010

YEAR	AIP	NAV 1000	S&P 500	NAV 1000	POTHOLE	T-BILL
1972	20.82%	1208	18.99%	1190		3.84
1973	18.78	1435	(14.69)	1015		6.93
1974	16.36	1670	(26.47)	746	(37.31)	8.00
1975	1.23	1690	37.23	1024		5.80
1976	20.08	2030	23.93	1269		5.08
1977	14.79	2330	(7.16)	1179		5.12
1978	15.39	2689	6.57	1256		7.18
1979	55.32	4176	18.61	1490		10.38

Table 5-6   AIP versus S&P 500, 1972–2010 *(Continued)*

YEAR	AIP	NAV	S&P 500	NAV	POTHOLE	T-BILL
1980	11.06	4638	32.50	1974		11.24
1981	(8.24)	4256	(4.92)	1877		14.71
1982	25.63	5347	21.55	2281		10.54
1983	4.99	5614	22.56	2796		8.90
1984	5.68	5933	6.27	2971		9.85
1985	18.69	7041	31.73	3914		7.72
1986	20.89	8512	18.67	4644		6.16
1987	6.05	9027	5.25	4888		5.47
1988	2.64	9265	16.61	5700		6.35
1989	8.06	10012	31.69	7507		8.37
1990	(4.11)	9600	(3.10)	7274		7.81
1991	15.48	11086	30.47	9490		5.60
1992	5.64	11,711	7.62	10,214		3.51
1993	17.96	13,814	10.08	11,243		2.90
1994	(1.78)	13,568	1.32	11,391		3.90
1995	15.97	15,735	37.58	15,672		5.60
1996	9.92	17,296	22.96	19,271		5.21
1997	4.90	18,143	33.36	25,699		5.26
1998	(1.76)	17,824	28.58	33,044		4.86
1999	(4.17)	17,082	21.04	39,997		0.68
2000	14.06	19,484	(9.10)	36,357		5.89
2001	6.13	20,678	(11.89)	32,034		3.83
2002	15.74	23,933	(22.10)	24,955	**(37.61)**	1.65
2003	19.49	28,598	28.68	32,112		1.02
2004	14.91	32,863	10.88	35,605		1.20
2005	12.58	36,997	4.91	37,354		2.98
2006	19.82	44,328	15.79	43,252		4.80
2007	8.85	48,250	5.49	45,626		4.66
2008	(2.82)	46,891	(37.00)	28,745	**(37.00)**	1.60
2009	13.57	53,256	26.46	36,350		0.10
2010	22.27	65,116	15.06	41,824		0.12

Table 5-6   AIP versus S&P 500, 1972–2010 *(Continued)*

	AIP	S&P 500
CMPD RETURN	*11.30*	*10.05*
T-Bill Return	5.56	5.56
Excess Return	5.74	4.49
Standard Deviation	11.17	18.33
Average. Underperformance	(1.99)	(5.10)
G/P ratio	2.88	0.88
Worst Drawdown	(8.24)	(37.61)
2nd Worst Drawdown	(5.85)	(37.31)
No. of Years Outperform T-Bill	26	26

THE PROPERTY MARKET

The third peg to our wealth-generating machine is the property market, both residential and commercial real estate. It is, by far, the largest alternative repository of wealth, that is, savings that usually will not be rechanneled directly back into productive investment. Furthermore, the underlying fundamentals of this asset class differ from those of stocks. At times, the real estate market attracts enough attention to interfere with the free flow of capital into productive investments. The National Association of Real Estate Investment Trusts (NAREIT), under the auspices of the FTSE, a company that specializes in index calculations, coowned by the London Stock Exchangeand the *Financial Times.*, has put together a price series of equity REITs, which includes all tax-qualified real estate trusts that are listed on the New York Stock Exchange and the Nasdaq, dating back to the beginning of 1972. REITs will be our third alternative asset class; its prices and returns were also included in Table 5-5.

ALTERNATIVE MARKET CLASSES TO THE RESCUE

Each of these three alternative investments (gold, long-term Treasuries, and REITs) composes a distinct asset class tied to one of the basic foundational blocks of our "wealth-generating machine." Ordinarily, the stream of capital into these areas is not enough to interfere with money flows into productive business ventures. However at times, the normal flow of money into productive investments is disrupted and one of these three alternative asset sectors may attract a larger-than-usual capital surge.

Given this potentially disruptive relationship, we could expect these three alterative investments to be "negatively correlated" to equities, meaning that when stocks are in a funk, one or more of the other asset classes are likely to step forward and carry the day. We will skip the mathematically arcane formulas for detecting negative correlation and substitute a simpler one.

- Each alternative investment can be compared with the stock market on an annual basis. We note the number of years when they move in an opposite direction—that is, one displays a positive return while the other is in the red.
- Each year of divergence can be considered a negative correlation, and we add them all up.
- We then divide that number by the total number of years observed, to get a ratio: negative correlation to total years (NC/TY).

Percentages above 20 percent seem to display a decent amount of negative correlation. Ratios above 33 percent appear to indicate a high degree of negative correlation. As we have seen in Table 5-3, each of these three alternative investments displayed anywhere from mild, in the case of REITs, to substantial, in the case of gold and long-term Treasuries, negative correlation to the S&P 500.

On the other hand, the Morgan Stanley Capital International Index of Developed Stock Markets (MSCI), the Morgan Stanley Capital International Index of Emerging Markets (EEM), the Nasdaq, and the Russell 2000 Index (an index of smaller cap U.S. stocks) did not show nearly as much independence from the S&P 500.

But that is not all. Each of these three assets also showed considerable negative correlation to each other (see Table 5-4). Take gold, for instance: It had 21 negative correlations to long-term Treasuries and it also zigged an additional 19 times when REITs zagged. That's a total of 40 negative correlations from 78 observations (39 observations of gold to each of its two co-pieces, Treasuries and REITs, totaling 78), and it comes out to a negative correlation ratio of approximately 51 percent. (*Note:* Long-term Treasuries easily beat out intermediate government bonds in negative correlation. Also the negative correlation of 54 percent of long-term Treasuries to gold (21/39 = 54 percent) goes a long way to explaining G/T's excellent performance.)

The 1972–2010 returns for each of the three alternative asset classes are presented in Table 5-5.

As we can see, both gold and long-term Treasuries had compounded returns well below that of the S&P 500, while REITs did considerably better. It also becomes apparent why gold was confined to the back alley of the investment world. How could investors, viewing an asset in the process of chalking up an ugly average underperformance number of (7.18), an off-the-chart worst drawdown of (53.41) percent, and a miserly G/P ratio of 0.53, which was way below both of the other two assets and the S&P 500, not have been spooked out?

If we simply averaged the compounded return of the three alternative investments we would get a figure of 9.94 percent, which was about 0.11 percent below the S&P 500 during that same 39-year time frame. And that was certainly nothing to shout about.

However, when we put the three alternative assets together, one-third apiece, and rebalance yearly, the story becomes quite interesting. (See Table 5-7.)

Table 5-7   Combined Investment A/B Portfolio

YEAR	INVESTMENT A	NAV 1000	INVESTMENT B	NAV 1000	50%A/50%B	NAV 2000
1	(25.0%)	$750	55.0%	$1550	15.0%	$2300
2	45.0	1087.5	(25.0)	1162.5	10.0	2530
CMPD Return	4.28%		7.82%		12.47%	

This alternative investment portfolio (AIP) thumped a stand-alone S&P 500 investment. According to investment folklore, risk and return are related; the greater the return, the more the risk. Yet this did not happen. AIP's 11.30 percent compounded return was more than a full percent above the S&P 500's 10.05 percent return, producing a nearly 56 percent greater total dollar return than the S&P 500 over the 39-year period. Meanwhile AIP's AU of (1.99) was only 39 percent of S&P 500's AU of (5.10), implying it was about 61 percent less risky. (Its standard deviation suggests about 39 percent less risk). We, in fact, got the proverbial "free lunch." AIP was a win/win, in that both sides of the risk/reward equation improved. And, of course, AIP's gain-to-pain ratio of 2.88 swamped the S&P 500's G/P ratio of 0.88. If that wasn't enough, AIP's very worst annual compounded loss of (8.24) percent made the S&P 500's loss of (37.6) percent seem elephantine during the same time frame. There were no forced visits to the torture chambers. AIP did not fall into a deep pothole during this time span. This is another case of the whole (the three pieces together) producing an outcome that was much greater than the sum of the parts.

Why the Combined Portfolio Return Was Higher

Yet how was this alternative investment portfolio able to produce a return considerably higher than the compounded gains of two of its three components, rather than a return closer to its 9.94 average? To see how combining negatively correlated investments into a portfolio and rebalancing them annually can produce a return significantly higher than its individual components, let's take a look at a hypothetical two-year return from a portfolio containing investments A and B, each starting with $1000 (Table 5-8).

Table 5-8   Alternative Portfolio During 3 Deep Potholes

	S&P 500	AIP	COMBINED RETURN
1973–1974	(37.3) %	+38.2%	+0.45
2000–2002	(37.6)	+40.0	+1.20
2008	(37.0)	(2.8)	(19.90)

Investment A had imaginary returns of (25.0) percent and 45.0 percent, which produced a two-year compounded return of 4.28 percent. Investment B's hypothetical returns were 55 percent and (25.0) percent over the same two-year span, which yielded a compounded return of 7.82 percent. What happened was that after year one, A's $1000 original investment had dwindled to just $750, while B's total had increased to $1550. The combined portfolio was worth $2300, a 15 percent return for the portfolio in year one.

Without rebalancing, A's second year 45 percent gain, based on its beginning $750 amount, would have amounted to only $337.50, or $750 × 45%, while B's 25 percent loss on its $1550 beginning-of-the-year amount would have been $387.50, or $1550 × (25%). The net effect of a $337.50 gain less a $387.50 loss would have been a $50 net loss, and the combined portfolio would have ended year two with $2250 and a compound return of 6.07 percent, just about midway between A and B.

Now let's rebalance and see how it changes the outcome. After year one, $400 was shifted from Investment B to Investment A so that each investment began the second year with $1150. This paid off as A's 45 percent return was now able to generate a $517.50 dollar return to the portfolio. Meanwhile, B's (25) percent loss subtracted only $287.50 from the portfolio. The net effect was a combined profit of $230, and that resulted in a 10 percent return, upping the prior year's NAV of $2300 to $2530. The compounded two-year return now clocks in at a very respectable 12.47 percent. Get the picture?

AIP DURING THE THREE DEEP POTHOLES

Without rebalancing, climbing out of a deep drawdown hole can be a big problem. For example, following a 50 percent losing year, it takes a 100 percent profit to get you back to even. However, redistributing some of a co-investment's winnings to the loser can act as a rope ladder, making the climbing out process easier and faster. And that is what happened within the AIP.

We now have a three-pieced (AIP) that outperformed the S&P 500 during the past 39 years while subjecting followers to substantially less risk. And the frosting on that tasty cake was an admirable performance during the three deep S&P 500 potholes that occurred in that time span, more than offsetting the S&P 500 loss in two of them. See Table 5-9.

While bonds have long been considered a legitimate alternative to equities, REITs and gold are relative newcomers to the alternative asset field, both beginning their investment scorecard in 1972. However, most investors are familiar with our history of rising property prices and are likely to be fairly comfortable holding REIT investments.

Table 5-9   Gold and Treasury (G/T) Passive Portfolio

YEAR	GOLD	20-YEAR TREASURIES	COMBINED (G/T)	NAV 1000
1972	+48.75%	+5.69%	+27.22%	1272
1973	72.96	(1.11)	35.93	1729
1974	66.15	4.35	35.25	2339
1975	(24.80)	9.20	(7.80)	2156
1976	(4.10)	16.75	6.33	2293
1977	22.64	(0.69)	10.98	2544
1978	37.01	(1.18)	17.92	3000
1979	131.33	(1.23)	65.05	4952
1980	12.76	(3.95)	4.41	5170
1981	(32.57)	1.86	(15.36)	4376
1982	14.94	40.36	27.65	5586
1983	(16.31)	0.65	(7.83)	5149
1984	(19.38)	15.48	(1.95)	5048
1985	6.00	31.97	18.49	5982
1986	18.97	24.53	21.75	7283
1987	24.51	(2.71)	10.90	8076
1988	(15.24)	9.67	(2.79)	7851
1989	(2.85)	18.11	7.63	8450
1990	(3.11)	6.18	1.54	8580
1991	(8.56)	19.30	5.37	9041
1992	(5.73)	8.05	1.16	9146
1993	15.98	18.24	17.11	10,711
1994	(0.74)	(7.77)	(4.26)	10,255
1995	0.98	31.67	16.33	11,929
1996	(4.59)	(0.93)	(2.76)	11,600
1997	(21.41)	15.85	(2.78)	11,277
1998	(0.83)	13.06	6.12	11,967
1999	1.08	(8.96)	(3.94)	11,495
2000	(5.65)	21.48	7.92	12,405
2001	0.75	3.70	2.23	12,681

Table 5-9   Gold and Treasury (G/T) Passive Portfolio *(Continued)*

YEAR	GOLD	20-YEAR TREASURIES	COMBINED (G/T)	NAV
2002	25.57	17.84	21.71	15,434
2003	19.89	1.45	10.67	17,081
2004	4.65	8.51	6.58	18,204
2005	17.77	7.81	12.79	20,533
2006	23.20	1.19	12.20	23,037
2007	32.36	9.88	21.12	27,902
2008	3.41	25.87	14.64	31,987
2009	27.63	(14.90)	6.37	34,023
2010	28.72	10.14	19.43	40,634

COMBINED (G/T)	
CMPD Return	+9.96
T-Bill Return	+ 5.56
Excess Return	+ 4.40
Standard Deviation	+14.78
Average. Underperformance	(3.39)
G/P Ratio	+1.30
Worst Drawdown	(15.36)
2nd Worst Drawdown	(7.83)
Outperform T-Bill, No. of Yrs.	24

Gold, on the other hand, has had a pretty ugly long-term history. While a goodly number of sophisticated investors have come to appreciate gold's investment merits, the general investment public probably still has a long way to go before they are fully comfortable with assigning the yellow metal a prominent role in their investment portfolios. And that could well be a net plus to investors in alternative assets, as it could mean it may take quite a while before the general public catches on to gold's investment potential.

Yet, in a world of paper money, large-scale government indebtedness, extraordinary government deficits, and the potential for increasing inflationary headwinds down the road, gold's prospects to remain an alive, perhaps a very alive, asset are quite good. And its robust performance during the recent disinflationary period would seem to back this up.

In the next chapter, we try to hook AIP up with the S&P 500 to create a passive combined asset portfolio.

CHAPTER 6

A Passive Combined Asset Portfolio Strategy

We are ready to merge the alternative investment portfolio (AIP) with an S&P 500 investment portfolio to create a passive combined asset (PCA) portfolio. The two leading choices for assembling a portfolio that make the most sense are a either a 50/50 AIP/S&P 500 split or equally divided among all four asset classes: S&P 500, REITs, long-term Treasuries, and gold.

My choice is an equal split among the four assets. The AIP itself had a negative correlation to the S&P 500 of 23 percent. See Table 5-6. However, gold and long-term Treasuries had far greater negative correlations both to each other and to the S&P 500—46 percent and 38 percent, respectively. See Table 5-3. Each asset class represents different functions within our wealth-generating system. By including each asset class individually and equally, we get the most impact from asset-class variation.

In Table 6-1, we divide the four asset classes equally and rebalance at the end of each calendar year. The overall results are compared to the other portfolios and their individual components in Table 6-2.

As you can see, this passive combined asset portfolio's 11.34 percent compounded return bettered the S&P 500 return by more than 1 percent over the 1972–2010 period. Its total dollar return was also about 58 percent greater.

Table 6-1   Passive Combined Asset (PCA) Portfolio: Total Four Asset Classes, 1972–2010

YEAR	S&P 500	REITs	LONG-TERM TREASURIES	GOLD	PCA	NAV 1000
1972	+18.99	+8.01	+5.69	+48.75	+20.36	1204
1973	(14.69)	(15.52)	(1.11)	72.96	+10.41	1329
1974	(26.47)	(21.40)	4.35	66.15	+5.65	1404
1975	37.23	19.30	9.20	(24.80)	+10.23	1548
1976	23.93	47.59	16.75	(4.10)	+21.04	1873
1977	(7.16)	22.42	(0.69)	22.64	+9.30	2048
1978	6.57	10.34	(1.18)	37.01	+13.19	2318
1979	18.61	35.86	(1.23)	131.33	+46.14	3387
1980	32.50	24.37	(3.95)	12.76	+16.42	3943
1981	(4.92)	6.00	1.86	(32.57)	(7.41)	3651
1982	21.55	21.60	40.36	14.94	+24.61	4550
1983	22.56	30.64	0.65	(16.31)	+9.38	4976
1984	6.27	20.93	15.48	(19.38)	+5.83	5266
1985	31.73	19.10	30.97	6.00	+21.95	6422
1986	18.67	19.16	24.53	18.97	+20.34	7728
1987	5.25	(3.64)	(2.71)	24.51	+5.85	8180
1988	16.61	13.49	9.67	(15.24)	+6.13	8682
1989	31.69	8.92	18.11	(2.85)	+13.97	9895
1990	(3.10)	(15.41)	6.18	(3.11)	(3.86)	9513
1991	30.47	35.70	19.30	(8.56)	+19.23	11,342
1992	7.62	14.59	8.05	(5.73)	+6.14	12,038
1993	10.08	19.65	18.24	15.98	+15.99	13,963
1994	1.32	3.17	(7.77)	(0.74)	(1.01)	13,823
1995	37.58	15.27	31.67	0.98	+21.37	16,777
1996	22.96	35.27	(0.93)	(4.59)	+13.18	18,988
1997	33.36	20.26	15.85	(21.41)	+12.02	21270
1998	28.58	(17.50)	13.06	(0.83)	+5.83	22,508
1999	21.04	(4.62)	(8.96)	1.08	+2.13	22,988
2000	(9.10)	26.37	21.48	(5.65)	+8.27	24,890
2001	(11.89)	13.93	3.70	0.75	+1.63	25,294
2002	(22.10)	3.82	17.84	25.57	+6.28	26,883
2003	28.68	37.13	1.45	19.89	+21.79	32,740

Table 6-1   Passive Combined Asset (PCA) Portfolio: Total Four Asset Classes, 1972–2010 (Continued)

YEAR	S&P 500	REITS	LONG-TERM TREASURIES	GOLD	PCA	NAV
2004	10.88	**31.58**	8.51	4.65	+13.90	37,291
2005	4.91	12.16	7.81	17.77	+10.66	41,267
2006	15.79	**35.06**	1.19	**23.20**	+18.81	49,031
2007	5.49	(15.69)	9.88	**32.36**	+8.01	52,958
2008	**(37.00)**	**(37.73)**	**25.87**	3.41	(11.37)	46,939
2009	**26.46**	**27.99**	(14.90)	**27.63**	+16.79	54,822
2010	15.06	**27.95**	10.14	**28.72**	**+20.47**	66,044

	PCA
CMPD Return	+11.34
T-Bill Return	5.56
Excess Return	5.78
Standard Deviation	10.16
Average Underperformance	(1.62)
G/P Ratio	3.57
Worst Drawdown	(11.37)
2nd Worst Drawdown	(7.41)
Outperform T-Bill, no. of Years	30

Table 6-2   PCA versus Other Passive Portfolios, 1972–2010

	CMPD RETURN	ER	AU	G/P	WDD	ST. DEV.
PCA	**11.34%**	**5.78%**	**(1.62)**	**3.57**	**(11.37)**	**10.16**
S&P 500	10.05	4.49	(5.10)	0.88	(37.61)	18.33
60/40 SB	9.60	4.04	(2.94)	1.37	(19.63)	11.54
AIP	11.30	5.74	(1.99)	2.88	(8.24)	11.17
Long-Term Treasuries	8.46	2.90	(3.43)	0.85	(14.90)	12.00
Gold	9.34	3.78	(7.18)	0.53	(53.41)	30.09
REITs	12.01	6.45	(4.74)	1.36	(47.50)	18.94

More importantly, the PCA portfolio's risk profile was in another league from that of the S&P 500. An average underperformance of (1.62), just 32 percent of the S&P 500's AU of (5.10), suggested it was 68 percent less risky. The PCA gain-to-pain ratio of 3.57 was more than four times greater than the S&P 500's G/P ratio of 0.88. The PCA 's worst drawdown of (11.37) percent, compared to the S&P 500's three falloffs of (37.00) percent or more, was sure to leave buy-and-hold investors envious. Furthermore, the PCA also beat the risk-free long-term T-Bill during 30 years, while the S&P 500 did so in only 26 of the years.

The PCA portfolio also significantly outpaced the 60/40 stock/bond strategy. The PCA's compounded return was more than 1.5 percent greater, while its AU ratio suggested it was only 45 percent less risky. Additionally, the PCA's gain-to-pain ratio of 1.37 was more than two and a half times the G/P ratio of the 60/40 stock/bond strategy.

Interestingly, had we chosen the one-half AIP/one-half S&P 500 split, the results would not have been all that much different (see Table 6-3). The compounded return would have been only slightly lower at 11.16 percent, although the journey would have been considerably rockier. The portfolio's AU of (2.47) was a good deal higher, and its G/P ratio of 2.27 fell way short; poorer results, but still considerably better than a straight S&P 500 investment.

Table 6-3   S&P 500 versus AIP 50/50, 1972–2010

YEAR	S&P 500	NAV $1000	AIP	COMBINED	NAV 1000
1972	18.99	1190	+20.80	+19.89	1199
1973	(14.69)	1015	18.76	2.03	1223
1974	(26.47)	746	16.33	(5.07)	1161
1975	37.23	1024	1.23	19.23	1385
1976	23.93	1269	20.06	21.99	1689
1977	(7.16)	1179	14.77	3.80	1753
1978	6.57	1256	15.37	10.97	1945
1979	18.61	1490	55.33	36.97	2665

Table 6-3   S&P 500 versus AIP 50/50, 1972–2010 (Continued)

YEAR	S&P 500	NAV	AIP	COMBINED	NAV
1980	32.50	1974	11.07	21.78	3245
1981	(4.92)	1877	(8.24)	(6.58)	3032
1982	21.55	2281	25.63	23.59	3747
1983	22.56	2796	4.97	13.76	4262
1984	6.27	2971	5.77	6.02	4519
1985	31.73	3914	18.70	25.21	5658
1986	18.67	4644	20.86	19.76	6776
1987	5.25	4888	6.07	5.66	7160
1988	16.61	5700	2.67	9.64	7850
1989	31.69	7507	8.00	19.84	9408
1990	(3.10)	7274	(4.10)	(3.60)	9069
1991	30.47	9490	15.47	22.97	11,152
1992	7.62	10,214	5.60	6.61	11,889
1993	10.08	11,243	17.96	14.02	13,556
1994	1.32	11,391	(1.80)	(0.24)	13,524
1995	37.58	15,672	16.00	26.79	17,147
1996	22.96	19,271	10.53	16.74	20,017
1997	33.36	25,699	4.90	19.13	23,846
1998	28.58	33,044	(1.73)	13.42	27,046
1999	21.04	39,997	(4.17)	8.43	29,327
2000	(9.10)	36,357	14.07	2.48	30,054
2001	(11.89)	32,034	6.10	(2.90)	29,182
2002	(22.10)	24,955	15.73	(3.19)	28,251
2003	28.68	32,112	19.46	24.07	35,051
2004	10.88	35,605	14.90	12.89	39,570
2005	4.91	37,354	12.53	8.72	43,020
2006	15.79	43,252	19.83	17.81	50,681
2007	5.49	45,626	8.87	7.18	54,321
2008	(37.00)	28,745	(2.83)	(19.92)	43,500
2009	26.46	36,350	13.57	20.01	52,205
2010	15.06	41,824	22.27	18.66	61,946

Table 6-3   S&P 500 versus AIP 50/50, 1972–2010 *(Conntinued)*

	S&P 500	*AIP*	*COMBINED 50/50*
CMPD Return	10.05%	11.30	11.16
T-Bill Return	5.56	5.56	5.56
Excess Return	4.49	5.74	5.60
Standard Deviation	18.33	11.17	11.46
Average Underperformance	(5.10)	(1.99)	(2.47)
G/P Ratio	0.88	2.88	2.27
Worst Drawdown	(37.61)	(8.24)	(19.92)

PCA PORTFOLIO'S BIOLOGICAL FOUNDATION

This passive four-piece PCA portfolio—including gold, long-term (L-T) Treasuries, REITs, and the S&P 500—is based on a firm biological concept. By providing investors with three additional asset classes, or design variations, it allows investors a greater chance to find the "fitter" asset class to respond to the investment climate of the day. And it did what it was supposed to do, that is, find "fit" asset classes more readily than a single asset investment strategy. If you look closely at Table 6-1, you will notice that at least one of the alternatives beat out the S&P 500 during 30 of the 39 years, and two or more did so in 20 years. Also, at least one of the four pieces turned in a 20 percent, or better, performance (in **bold**) in 30 of the 39 years. That was in stark contrast to the 6 years when one or more of the four pieces registered a loss of 20 percent or more. (By the way, in four of those years, the PCA still finished in the black).

Furthermore, there was not a single year in which all four pieces went negative at the same time. However, all four were up together during 11 years. Three or more component pieces were positive during 26 of the 39 years, or 67 percent of the time (see Table 6-4).

Table 6-4   Positive to Negative Composition of the Four Components

NUMBER OF POSITIVE COMPONENTS	NUMBER OF YEARS	PERCENTAGE
4	11	28
3	16	41
2	10	26
1	2	5
0	0	0

All in all, by providing variation, the PCA portfolio delivered a robust long-term total return punch, while allowing investors to offset a loss in one, or sometimes even two or three, of the asset classes. This portfolio certainly seems far more "adaptive" than a straight S&P 500 strategy.

VARIATION BEATS THE S&P 500 B&H PORTFOLIO

This portfolio plainly suggests that investing in a diversity of asset classes makes a fundamental contribution to system performance, much as variation does in evolution. Investors can place a bet on the continued long-term growth of our dynamic economic system, while also betting on fluctuations in our financial system and changes in the property market. All major bases are covered.

Going forward, this plain-vanilla portfolio could easily be implemented by using four exchange-traded funds (ETFs): SPY, GLD, TLT, and VNQ, which represent the S&P 500, gold, long-term Treasuries, and REITs, respectively. Naturally, this primitive asset allocation can be tinkered with a bit, perhaps adding the Morgan Stanley Emerging Market (EEM) Index along with the Nasdaq 100 Index (QQQ) for a portion of the equity amount. Also, either the gold and or the long-term Treasuries components could be enlarged or lessened a bit. However, it is unlikely that the results would change all that much.

Keep in mind, although the precise shape of the future is unknowable, we can deploy our assets in a way that is more likely to capture the knowable possibilities. The PCA portfolio, although it was actively designed around the evolutionary concept of variation, is a passive, buy-and-hold investment strategy. We now switch gears and see if we can develop an active strategy built around another important evolutionary CAS concept, the natural fluctuations that occur within living systems, and use it to beat this passive strategy.

PART 3

FLUCTUATIONS: THE KEY TO UNDERSTANDING COMPLEX ADAPTIVE SYSTEMS

When we leave the world of passive investing, we cross an important threshold. We are no longer attempting to apply long-tested rules, based on past outcomes, to properly position our-selves for a future we assume will be pretty much like the past.

On the other side of the threshold, we try to actively "guess" the future, and that is a daunting task; many think it is an act of futility. The reason is that we are dealing with a "living system"—something that Newtonians aren't very good at.

But we do have something that Newtonians don't have, that is, an alternative Darwinian worldview, which includes "complex adaptive systems." And a central feature of these systems is their oscillating up-and-down trends. When a critical level is breached, a significant change—a phase transition—takes place in the func-tioning of these systems.

In the following two chapters, I will lay out the complex nature of investment markets.

CHAPTER 7

Trends: The Central Feature of Our Investment And Economic World

Investment markets and the economy are joined at the hip, forming a great wealth-creating system that we celebrate as free-market capitalism. Its central feature is *fluctuation*, which alternates between expansion and contraction, or bull and bear markets, in trendlike movements. One can make an unmistakable observation: Since the dawn of capitalism, stock market history has been a long roller-coaster ride of ups and downs, bubbles and busts, and manias and panics.

Yet the idea of cyclical fluctuating markets is a hard sell, primarily because most in the investment community—ordinary investors, investment academicians, and Wall Street professionals—have partnered up in a subconscious conspiracy to cover up the bitter phase of the cycle. To them, the central feature in both our stock market and the economy is a long-term rising trend—small deviations, which we continually try to correct, are allowed. They are starry-eyed about capitalism's remarkable ability to produce increasingly higher levels of affluence and prosperity. They think a society that has mastered nature should be able to underwrite higher and higher levels of corporate earning power, which surely will outlast the life spans of us all. The investment community's message is loud and clear: Take advantage of this super trend of expanding business profits by buying stocks and stick with them over the long haul, *ignoring* annoying bear market potholes along the way.

But is the central feature of our wealth-generating machine a super long-term trend that continuously points up or is the central feature the up-and-down fluctuations of the marketplace?

KEYNES'S THOUGHTS ON INVESTING

Let's ask John Maynard Keynes, probably the twentieth century's most respected economist, who was also an accomplished investor with an unusually acute understanding of how markets functioned. Keynes, who was also a British lord, was skeptical of people's ability to analyze investments. According to him, "the outstanding fact is the extreme precariousness of the basis of knowledge on which our estimates … have to be made. … If we speak frankly, we have to admit the basis of this knowledge … amounts to little and sometimes nothing."[1] Keynes thought people, when facing an uncertain future, copy what others are doing. They run with the crowd, so as to avoid being left the odd man out. But they can't just run like a herd of cattle after some lead steers. So they disguise this uncertainty from themselves by resorting to "conventions … pretty, polite techniques, one of which is (even) economics itself." It provides them with the courage to overcome the paralysis of uncertainty.

Furthermore, Keynes believed any view of the future based on "so flimsy a foundation" is liable to "sudden and violent changes. … New fears and hopes will, without warning, take charge of human conduct … the market will be subject to (alternating) waves of optimistic and pessimistic sentiment, which are unreasoning yet, in a sense, legitimate where no solid base exists for a reasonable calculation."

Today, we would call Keynes's "reasonable calculations" *fundamental analysis*, a popular method of delving into the relevant information, data and statistics, pertaining to an investment so as to calculate its real "value." Presumably, investors who acquire the skill of ascertaining correct values will be able to load up their portfolios with securities currently selling at a discount to "presumed" value and thus outperform the market. This traditional method of investing is favored by many, if not most, buy-and-hold–type investors, who have already made the decision to continually own a basket of securities.

Yet Keynes didn't seem to have much respect for this method. Listen closely to the British lord's message, and you hear, "the basis of knowledge on which our estimates ... have to be made ... amounts to little and sometimes nothing," and the coup de grâce, "no solid basis exists for a reasonable calculation." The clear implication is that the knowledge of fundamentals, statistics, and data tells us very little.

The case against the fundamental/statistical approach follows:

- The approach is often based on models of economic relationships derived in an environment that is already disappearing in our rearview mirror. Journalist David Leonhardt, writing in the *New York Times* op-ed page in June 2009, claimed President Obama's economists made an avoidable mistake by relying on "the same forecasting models that had completely failed to see the crisis coming. ... These models ... are notoriously bad at forecasting turning points because they are based on an assumption that the recent past will more or less repeat itself."[2]
- In a dynamic economy such as ours, statistics have a data-collecting problem. Most data derives meaning by comparison to some prior number (e.g., gross domestic product (GDP) is up 4 percent from the prior quarter, or retail sales are down 2 percent from a year ago). But such comparisons can be way off the mark due to the difficulty in estimating the formation of new companies and the demise of established firms. Just think of the fairly recent arrival of the Internet and all the new electronic start-ups popping up daily. The statistics from such new arrivals are not properly incorporated into our public and private surveys until a fresh census is taken, which might be years away. That often leads to inaccurate reports which are only cleaned up, months or

sometimes even years later, by revisions, some of which are substantial.

- If that isn't enough, Keynes claimed, investors don't know which information is relevant. There is a great deal of—perhaps too much—information floating around. Much of it falls into the category we call "noise," meaningless chatter masquerading as the real thing. And that, no doubt, confuses many investors.

This is not to say good data or information is always irrelevant. Important information not available to most others can be quite useful. The problem is that today we have an information democracy wherein most of the good stuff is quickly disseminated throughout the investment community and will already be priced into the market by the time ordinary investors get wind of it. In short, the usefulness of fundamental/statistical information is quite limited. So let's take the British lord's other observation to heart and turn our attention to trying to make sense of those waves of "optimistic and pessimistic sentiment," which in fact are the up and down bull and bear markets we talk of. This up-and-down cyclical pattern may very well be the illusive key necessary to understand a living system.

FLUCTUATIONS: BULL AND BEAR MARKETS

Bull and bear markets are adaptive responses to a significant change in the external environment, usually the economy. When an unexpected robust and sustained business expansion occurs, human agents adopt a risk-taking behavioral pattern, which becomes the building blocks for a bull market. On the flip side, an unanticipated economic or financial trauma transforms agent behavior into a cautious, risk-avoiding mode, which plays out as a bear market. This process—from environmental shift to bull or bear market—occurs in a symmetrical, trendlike pattern, similar to a flock of birds arranging itself in a coordinated fight pattern.

Oh, come on, Stoken. Are you really trying to tell us that humans act like birds?

Well ... yes ... in a sense.

There are two unseen, but important, links that guide human agents in an adaptive response to some external event. The first is a *transmitter*, which connects the external environment to a corollary human behavioral pattern and at the same time spawns a second link. The second link is the *attractor*, whose function is to finish the job by drawing in the goodly number of agents who are slower to adopt the proper behavioral response.

The transmitter results from a mass change in an agent's perception of risk from more to less, or vice versa. Unexpected external events, such as a period of robust economic expansion or a serious destruction of wealth, serve as important lessons of pleasure or pain. Those events which make our wealth-creating system appear either more benign or more dangerous, turn on or off our sensor to danger that we humans share with other animals. Changes in these risk perceptions spread throughout the investment community and, in so doing, act as an unseen current running beneath the path of all bull and bear markets, guiding their course.

When people view their economic world as less risky, "animal spirits" are aroused and channeled directly into risk-taking behavior. On the other hand, a perception of high risk sends out a signal for agents to retreat into a cautious, risk-avoiding mode. Of course, not every shift in risk perceptions is significant. Only those that breach a *critical level*—which usually can be monitored by keeping an eye glued to stock prices—are likely to connect an external event to a corresponding mass behavioral response, marking the beginning of a self-feeding bull or bear market.

Shortly after risk perceptions have fallen below this critical level—which occurs following a persistent rally of some duration in the stock market—the new *behavioral patterns*, the ways a significant number of agents are thinking and acting, start attracting attention. This situation introduces a new mini-culture into the business and investment community. This culture will spout new ideas, such as that taking a risk is now a legitimate activity and not reckless gambling; market falloffs are buying opportunities and not a sign to dump risky assets; and spending more of your income, sometimes even frivolously, does not label husbands or wives as "irresponsible."

Meanwhile, tales of business and investment success are told and retold. Plausible explanations for the persistence of the upward price trajectory are batted about. Soon the stories and explanations are woven together into a narrative. If the story fits into a world that appears to be less risky—stories with a bearish implication would be rejected out of hand—it resonates throughout the investment community, becoming widely accepted as a rationale or "Keynesian convention," legitimatizing the new insurgent culture, and becoming the attractor. These Keynesian conventions play the important cultural role of attracting agents who require more certainty before adopting a risk-taking mode of behavior by providing them with the courage to join into the new way of thinking and acting.

Although each bull market has its own narrative, there is a remarkable consistency about them in that all posit a "prosperous tomorrow" and the acceptance of a rising market becomes a matter of faith, which economists term "confidence." What had gone on before is made to seem inevitable. Agents, believing more of the same lies in store, commit to the rising market, providing a surge of energy to further fuel an ongoing trend that is continually hungry for new sources of power.

Following the Trend

Cultures also need heroes or leaders to provide examples for others to follow. This requirement is not difficult to fill, as there will always be a few agents who saw the bullish possibilities early on. Some are sure to be promoted to "lead steers," and other agent members of the herd will follow and take their opinions as gospel.

Keep in mind, there will be some events or pieces of information contrary to the main trend that are able to trip danger sensors in enough agents so as to set off a countertrend price move, but they do not provide compelling enough stories to become an attractor. In that case, you can count on the shift in risk perceptions to fall short of breaching the critical level necessary to trigger a self-feeding trend in the opposite direction. However, these countertrend price movements do interrupt the main trend and, as such, we call them *corrections*.

When external conditions call for it, the transmitter and the attractor leap into action to form an *adaptive network*, which relays cues throughout the agent population, prompting humans to change their behavior in a process that, though messier, resembles a flock of birds arranging its synchronized pattern of motion. Most, though not all, human agents join in a coordinated self-organizing movement, which we know as bull or bear market trends, which take on lives of their own.

The widespread adoption of a "pursuit of profit-and-pleasure" behavioral pattern sets in motion a phalanx of positive feedback loops, which stimulate the economy, setting it on a fast-growth track, while also injecting steroids into the stock market.

Profit-seeking agents invest or increase stakes in the stock market, create start-ups, and buy or expand existing businesses. Other agents, perhaps the less active, are satisfied to merely increase their pleasure by spending more and saving less. Members of both species think nothing of taking on additional debt to invest in businesses or shares on a stock exchange, bigger and better homes, and expensive consumer items.

THE VIRTUOUS CYCLE

Gains in one sector of business spill over to the next, creating a *virtuous cycle*. For example, some actors exploit the new innovations, forging new companies that offer a fresh set of goods and services. Of course, new equipment is required to set up their businesses, so orders for capital goods tick up. New workers are then needed, and in order to attract some from their current employers, higher wages are often required. This bolsters workers' confidence, many of whom rev up their spending habits, triggering more retail sales. More sales mean inventories need to be replenished, creating more orders to manufacturers. Earnings prospects for business firms brighten. Astute investors notice and bid up prices on the nation's stock exchanges. So what happens next?

You guessed it: Rising share prices inject another shot of adrenaline into entrepreneurs' already elevated "animal spirits," calling for the positive feedback loops to spin again, setting off another round of business expansion … and on and on, until a great many of those agents who have been hopelessly stuck in mind-sets wedded to the old culture are aroused from their stupor.

During this time, the continual lowering of risk perceptions and the growing acceptance of the new culture also induces more and more agents who had been in a cautious behavioral mode to move to a sideline position. Many await a stock market reaction or an air pocket in economic activity as opportunities to shift their behavioral pattern into risk-taking mode. This growing reserve army of fence-sitting agents, waiting for an advantageous time to join in, is the ongoing trend's ace in the hole. During these times, stock market breaks are fairly contained and economic slowdowns are soon followed by renewed economic vigor. Most forecasters and market analysts, however, haven't accounted for groups of new actors joining in to nip the correction in the bud, and thus the mildness of these setbacks surprises them, as does the robustness of the following business expansion. Hurriedly they revise estimates upward, only, in many cases, to see the reported figure come in still higher. Surprises during this climate—whether in business earnings, GDP, or employment numbers—are overwhelmingly of the pleasant variety.

Sure there will be business errors and mistakes along the way; they are a natural part of any living system that relies on trial and error as its essential learning tool. But in this vigorous business environment—wherein individuals and businesses still maintain large margins of safety in the form of savings and low debt-to-equity ratios, respectively —most mistakes will be easily corrected and only a few will become embedded in the economy as inconsequential sores on the back of a gargantuan elephant.

THE VICIOUS CYCLE

Flip the coin to perceptions of a dangerous business and investment world and "animal spirits" go into remission. Large numbers of people exchange a risk-taking habit for a cautious, risk-avoiding approach in their economic and financial dealings. The appetite to buy or own assets is lost; in fact, it is condemned as irresponsible gambling. A penny-pinching public marching under a banner spelling *THRIFT* won't show much interest in spending for nonessential consumer items, nor the chutzpah to borrow for anything beyond a modest home. The pursuit of security becomes their main focus, as most people seek to build greater margins of safety into personal balance sheets. A huge cloud of agent caution hangs over the economy and the stock market, which leads to business retrenchment, worker pink slips, eroding retail sales, and over on Wall Street, most probably, a bear market. This movement to perceptions of higher risk, during the down phase of the cycle, usually occurs quickly, because fear of danger seems to be a more powerful instinct than greed.

In these situations, we become caught up in a vicious cycle wherein negative feedback loops ensure that most surprises will be unpleasant. More times than not, earnings' forecasts are trimmed and yet some of the actual figures still fall short of the estimates by wide margins. In late October 2008, during one of the most vicious negative feedback loops in more than half a century, a composite of Wall Street analysts were forecasting an unusually large 26 percent year-over-year increase for the S&P 500's first-quarter 2009 earnings. Five months later, in late March 2009, as the first quarter was coming to a close, Thomson Reuters reported those expectations had flipped to a more than one-third falloff in earnings. And to those investors who relied on that "slight" miscalculation … lots of luck! The negative feedback loops won out.

DIRECTION OF FEEDBACK LOOPS

In this bull-and-bear market construct, the most important, repeat, *most important*, piece of information an investor can rely on, far surpassing the statistics or data, is the *direction* of the human behavioral patterns and their corresponding feedback loops. Although unquantifiable, these patterns provide an overwhelming force, which endows the prevailing trend with its continuity. Investors, by putting their faith in these feedback loops, are able to peer into the future with a reasonable degree of accuracy. A simple trend bet is, in fact, an educated guess as to the future direction of the feedback loops, and most of the time it will *"outsmart"* attempts by experts to decipher the complex and continually shifting relationships between the numerous interacting components.

Investors live in an error-prone Darwinian world wherein markets, like evolution, may be smarter than us all. Yet those markets have a central feature, which is the up-and-down oscillations that exert a powerful pull, drawing us into adopting a corresponding behavioral pattern. This pattern is a forced adaption, often at just the wrong time, after bull and bear trends are approaching their end point. And that can be another error.

FORCED VERSUS PREEMPTIVE ADAPTATION

However, there is a strategy to prevent being yanked around by markets: adopt an adaptive posture by developing your own search tool to identify the *critical levels* that mark the turn from bull to bear, and vice versa. In doing so, you can co-opt the market and shift your behavior *before* the market forces you to. Then chances are your personal error rate will be less. In this game of investment, he or she who makes fewer errors than most others typically wins.

The ability to be a bull or a bear, as the situation calls for, is an important quality for investment success. When done properly, or "good enough," you will have the forces of a living system and, the most important piece of information, the direction of the unquantifiable feedback loops operating on your side. The majority of the surprises will favor the direction you are betting on, and your picture of reality—the way the world works—is likely to be more acute, rendering you better able to respond to unforeseen changes, some of which become vast "upheavals." Furthermore, preemptive adaption will simplify the investment process by letting you escape much of the noise and thus cut through what could be forbidding complexity.

But there is more to the story of trends: sometimes, though not always, they become *too* popular, or overcrowded; too many agents enter into a risk-taking behavioral pattern, or an overwhelming majority of the participants adopt an ultracautious mind-set. When either situation occurs, opinions coalesce around a central thesis and the nature of the trend changes. That will be the subject of the next chapter.

CHAPTER 8

A Paradox in Our Investment and Economic World

It is widely recognized that the health of an ecological system is based upon a delicate balance between interacting plants, animals, and microorganisms. Yet few appreciate that an economy's ability to deliver sustained growth also depends upon a certain balance between risk takers and risk avoiders.

When a trend overextends itself, the crowd of risk takers becomes excessive and our wealth-creating system crosses into "bubble" territory. This place is one which sports a culture of over optimism; it differs markedly from a mere trend toward lower risk perceptions, which refers only to the direction of the change in the crowd's perceptions. A mass culture of over-optimism, on the other hand, means mind-sets have locked into a perception of a "risk-free" economic investment world. When agents lack all respect for risk, their critical-thinking powers turn to mush and they begin a march on the road to folly, changing the nature of the trend.

ENTERING BUBBLE TERRITORY

It is not easy to cross into bubble territory. Several preconditions are required. A persistent rise in the price of some asset must team up with a story that subtly guarantees investors a pot of gold at the end of its rainbow, for example, the Internet, with its promise to transform the structure of American business, or the price of homes, ordained to rise ad infinitum. When a parabolic rise takes place and the story is established, a rationale, or Keynesian convention, graduates into a full-fledged belief system able to attract enormous numbers of gullible people, who formerly had shown little interest in that asset, into joining our wealth-generating machine as risk takers in search of their very own "Golden Calf." Yet, gullible people are usually short of the financial resources necessary to play in those daredevil games.

The last requirement necessary for a successful crossover into bubble territory is a financial sector that is both willing and able to finance the newcomers with cheap and abundant credit—enabling them to join in with little up-front money to make their dreams come true.

When these conditions are met, the culture, with its new and compelling belief system, breaks out of its limited business and investment space and becomes a societywide phenomenon. Lead steers gain a national audience. During the bull market of the 1990s, for example, Abby Joseph Cohen and Bill Miller were singing the songs that investors were dancing to.

To make sure the new culture is able to seep into every nook and cranny of our society, an additional feature attaches to it. This factor is "psychic punishment," in the form of lost opportunities or marginalization, meted out to nonbelievers. If you refuse to believe, your chances for career advancement in a business organization, a banking institution, or a government bureaucracy, may dim. Academics, even those who enjoy secure tenure, also may pay a price, sometimes steep, for straying from the herd. Those who dare to question the prevailing doctrine may see chances for generous outside consulting work or speaking engagements at world-class seaside resorts, paying big bucks, evaporate. Skeptics, in general, are benched for poor cue reading.

During the great housing bubble of the early 2000s, people all along the line, from real estate brokers to lending agents, from rating agents to mortgage bundlers, including politicians

and even the chairman of the Federal Reserve System, obedi-
ently fell into line. Lawrence McDonald in his book, *A Colossal
Failure of Common Sense*, tells the story of Madelyn Antoncic, a
competent risk manager at Lehman Brothers, who had become
a housing bear by the end of 2006. Richard. Fuld, the former
chief executive officer of Lehman Brothers, was not thrilled and
at one meeting told her to "shut up"; soon after she was demoted
to a government relations post.[1]

Of course, when the bubble burst, a few select skeptics who
had stuck to their guns and had good enough public relations
skills to find an audience were lionized as prescient prophets and
promptly promoted to lead steers. Economist Nouriel Roubini
and financial commentator Marc Faber became dour conductors
of an orchestra that played Chopin's "Funeral March" relentlessly
throughout 2008.

The Dot-com Bubble

Sometime around the mid-1990s, America's wealth-creating
system crossed over into "bubble" territory. Wall Street had
recently introduced a series of financial innovations, such as
securitization—asset-backed securities—and a host of complex
derivative securities, which tracked the movement of other
financial instruments. They provided businesses with new and
improved devices to hedge risk in ways that could be widely
dispersed throughout our wealth-generating system. At the same
time, Wall Street banks recruited an army of Ph.D.'s in physics
and mathematics to provide a set of mathematical equations
that would allow bankers to calculate risk as a single number. Wall
Streeters put blind faith in those numbers, thinking they had
finally tamed the age-old nemesis, "risk." Shocks and mistakes
that formerly had provoked a financial crisis would now hardly
cause a ripple throughout our financial system.

As we entered bubble territory, Alan Greenspan, chairman
of the Federal Reserve Bank (the Fed), with only one hand on

the monetary wheel, was dazzling the business and investment community with a brilliant display of coordinating interest rates so as to keep our economy almost recession free from 1987 to 2000; there was only one brief one in 1990. And, waving his other hand like a true "Mr. Maestro," he was able to keep credit flowing freely into the economy. He was to become the first Fed chairman to reach "rock-star" status.

Waves of new spending, well beyond anything seen previously, sent business profits soaring and produced a surge of new energy, lighting up our economic scoreboard. At the center of this system stood the latest and sexiest innovation in recent memory, the Internet, with its promise to forever change the way business around the world was to be conducted. A dot-com craze spread across the nation as a once-in-a-lifetime chance to get in on the ground floor of geeky new Internet firms that appeared destined to become giant global enterprises. Even leading TV personalities, such as Lou Dobbs, left careers in journalism to seek out their own Internet fortune. No dot-com stock was too rich or sported a price/earnings ratio too outrageous to scare away buyers; nor was any Internet start-up considered too expensive to invest in. Why, in a matter of only a few years' time, sales would skyrocket and the purchase prices would be repaid many times over. Those high markers were, in fact, merely alerting us to those company's bright prospects.

Furthermore, dot-com euphoria had created a magical investment climate lifting the broad stock market to heights well beyond long recognized standards of value. Huge amounts of dollars were sloshing through our economic and investment community; it appeared as if new millionaires, some of them neighbors, were being minted by the minute. People by the thousands were leaving good-paying jobs to set up shop in their kitchens and dining rooms as day traders. Men and women sat glued to their TVs, all day long, listening to commentators breathlessly reporting each new high, every piece of bullish news, and any positive opinion. A couple of prominent economists wrote a best-selling investment book predicting that the Dow Jones Industrial Average would soon reach the hard-to-believe 36,000 level (appropriately titled *Dow 36,000: The New Strategy for Profiting from the Coming Rise in the Stock Market*), and surprisingly many people believed. In fact, in the zeitgeist of the late 1990s, those people who shied away from investing in the stock market were thought to be fools who truly didn't deserve to become rich.

Then in early 2000, the dot-com bubble burst. The Nasdaq Index, home for most of the dot-com wannabe global giants, crashed more than 77 percent from its high water mark, dragging the whole market down a chilling 49 percent and crippling millions of 401(k)'s. Interest in the stock market plummeted. In fact, many investors and businesspeople thought the whole post–1970s period of increasing wealth had come to an end … but, of course, they hadn't reckoned with "Mr. Maestro" sitting firmly in the nation's monetary seat, with his foot pressed down hard on the interest-rate pedal.

Mr. Greenspan knew what a burst bubble could do to an economy. He was well aware that Japan's bubble economy had been pricked in early 1990 and for the following 10 years, while the rest of the world was participating in the fabulous "get rich quick" 1990s, Japan's economy and equity market remained in the sewer as the country suffered a "lost decade." Greenspan was not about to let that happen to America on his watch. He kept that heavy foot affixed to the nation's monetary pedal and, just to make sure, he left it there even after he heard the country's economic engines humming.

Thanks to him—with a bit of help from the Bush administration in the form of steep tax cuts and a deliberate and unusual (for a Republican administration) increase in public spending—the economy was able to lift up off the runway. But to get it back into the rarefied atmosphere of the 1990s, we needed an exciting new story, a new group of participants with dollar signs in their eyes, and an even larger flow of credit to afford them the means to join in and provide the system with another jolt of electricity. Yet equity markets, which had disappointed so many, could no longer provide that narrative.

The Housing Bubble

Fortunately, there was another story, and it was a good one. Since the end of World War II, regardless of recession, inflation, or war, home prices had been on a one-way street, pointing up. Each generation had plunked down their 20 percent, or so, of a price that was more than what their parents had paid, and years later, when cash-in time came, they walked away from their closing session, pockets bulging with more money than they ever thought possible.

The new gullible participants: the large "bottom of the economic ladder" group of agents who had been denied entry into our wealth-creating system because their meager savings failed to qualify them for a mortgage. Could we find a way to invite that group to the party?

Of course, we could; since home prices were ordained to keep on rising, we could ramp up our credit facilities so that homes could be purchased almost totally on credit. Bankers created "subprime" loans, which required either no down payment or just an itty-bitty amount. A liar's feature in which no income documentation was needed was added shortly thereafter. It was a bold experiment to bring lower-income people into the nation's wealth-generating machine, while, at the same time, providing the new energy necessary to take our machine back onto the expressway to be driven at full speed. For quite a while, it certainly looked as if everyone was benefitting. Home prices soared and the economy boomed. People, rich and (formerly) poor, flocked to the nation's shopping malls, spending like there was no tomorrow.

Yet this souped-up economy had a voracious appetite for ever-increasing amounts of credit. With a snap of the fingers, an unregulated *shadow banking system*—non-bank institutions, such as outside mortgage lenders, broker-dealers, structured investment vehicles (SIVs), conduits, and hedge funds—magically appeared and poured immense amounts of new credit into the system. Meanwhile, banks decided to open up their credit spigots further and provide easy access to credit to nearly anyone displaying a financial pulse rate. They flooded the mail with offers of credit cards—new ones arriving almost daily.

By the late 2000s, the average American family had 13 credit cards. Recipients used them to break the constraint paychecks had long placed on their spending habits. Naturally, some thought those cards, which were seducing increasing numbers of poor and middle-class people to pile on loads of debt, were weapons of mass destruction aimed at consumers. The credit card companies shot back. Quite the contrary! They were a vote of confidence by the nation's leading banks that recipients had the wherewithal to repay. Saving rates slowed to a dribble and after a while, those rates weren't even able to register a heartbeat.

At the same time, smiling home owners, both new and old, discovered that their dwellings could also serve as a personal ATM machine. Home and condo owners were able to self-finance—taking out new and cheaper mortgages—in order to purchase what they wanted, when they wanted, including even more homes.

A high-speed economy also requires "light-touch" regulators, who dare not slow the economy to a crawl. Bits of stardust from our high-flying economy had also fallen into the regulators' eyes, who, like most everyone else, were having trouble understanding the new financial innovations and their potential impact on the economy. They saw no need to play the villain by becoming picky with bold entrepreneurs who were driving in the fast lane. Why pull them over and issue a ticket just because they were driving 5 miles over the speed limit when traffic was flowing so smoothly and accident-free?

This was America from the mid-1990s until about 2007, and what a splendid time it was—all gain and (almost) no pain. Most agents were busy scurrying around in their own personal search for profit-and-pleasure opportunities. Who could fault them for being oblivious to the multiple cracks opening up under their feet, or for not recognizing they were following the rules of folly, rather than obeying the time-tested rules of prudence? Debt levels reached nosebleed heights, unprecedented levels of leverage attached to our economy and financial system, and share prices on the nation's stock exchanges reached giddy levels, yet almost no one appeared to care.

Nor did we pay attention to the fact that a proliferation of risk takers had intensified competition, making it more difficult for businesses to raise prices. Incidences of entrepreneurial failure edged up. As competition took on a more cutthroat edge, there was an increased amount of bending of the rules and blurring of the line between legal and illegal. The "animal spirits" now being aroused were, for the most part, no longer being channeled into honest-to-goodness risk taking. Instead they were diverted in a route that led from "greed" to reckless gambling and increasing amounts of corruption. The achievements of star business players—such as Bill Gates (Microsoft), Steve Jobs (Apple), and Jeff Bezos (Amazon)—were no longer capturing the fancy of the national media; instead it was becoming more interested in placing crowns of shame on shady business types, such as Bernie Ebbers (WorldCom), Jeff Skilling (Enron), and Dennis Kozlowski (Tyco). Nor did most people seem bothered by the fact that from 1995 to 2007 the average household income had grown by a measly, inflation-adjusted, 19 percent, while during that same time, the entry-level admission into the Forbes 400 richest families had increased by a whopping, inflation-adjusted, 180 percent. This disparity suggested the rich were the prime beneficiaries of this wealth explosion, with the middle and poorer classes divvying up the leftovers.

HAUNTED BY CATO'S SNARE

If this double bubble sounds reminiscent of the late 1920s, it should. We should remember, or should have remembered, the roller-coaster ride of financial terror that followed—a time of all pain and no gain. The words spoken by Cato, a Roman orator, 2000 years ago had come back to haunt us: "There must be a vast fund of stupidity in human nature, or else men would not be caught as they are, a thousand times over, by the same snares ... while they yet remember their past misfortunes, they go on to court and to encourage the causes to what they were owing, and which will again produce them."[3]

Imagine, just for a moment, some leading 1930's public official replying to Cato's ghost, "You were right, Mr. Cato. We got snared again. We're sorry, but because of you, we won't let it happen again." As far as I know, there is no record any such conversation ever took place. Nonetheless, we enlightened Newtonians, who are certainly anything but stupid, steered our post-1929, broken-down wealth-generating machine into fault-finding mode, so as to search out the errors and vilify those mistake makers responsible for that horrific calamity.

While to this day we still cannot agree on which error deserves the Oscar, there are four leading candidates:

- A Federal Reserve Board, peopled by a bunch of financial lightweights, who, as economist Milton Friedman pointed out, mistakenly tightened money supply growth when instead they should have eased it. At a conference in 2002 to honor Friedman, Ben Bernanke, who was to become the head of the Fed, apologized for those "wrongheaded" 1930s policies. "I would like to say to Milton ... regarding the Great Depression, you were right; we did it," he said. "We're very sorry. But, thanks to you we won't do it again."
- Tax increases imposed by both the Hoover and FDR administrations, with precision timing so as to topple a

fragile economy in the process of trying to struggle to
its feet.

- An ill-conceived rise in tariff rates, the infamous Smoot-
Hawley Tariff Act of 1930 that President Herbert Hoover,
disregarding the advice of many economists, signed.
- And finally at ground zero was a stock market "bubble,"
comparable to the great bubbles of the past. It too was
undergirded by a flood of cheap credit and a proliferation
of profit seekers, inspired by Edgar Lawrence Smith's
1924 best-selling book *Common Stocks as Long-Term
Investments*.[4] For the first time, a book offered up hard
evidence showing that during almost all past periods
surveyed common stocks had outperformed bonds,
which up to that time had been considered the superior
investment. Hordes of gullible citizens, proudly calling
themselves "speculators," invaded Wall Street, buying
shares on razor-thin margins (20 percent or less),
pushing prices way beyond any reasonable standard of
value. In October 1929, a date forever singed into our
history books, the bubble burst. It was to be that last
grain of sand, which toppled the whole pile, collapsing
the economic and financial edifice that had been erected
during the prior 30 years.

A new team of politicians settled in at the controls of the
nation's government and set out to restructure the economy so
that the above errors, and more, would not and could not be
repeated. Error makers, such as the financial wizards, whose crys-
tal balls had failed, were banished. A congressional committee of
blame surgeons deftly removed the reputations of those members
of the business community who had pushed beyond the edge of
the envelope, and some were shipped off to Sing Sing prison.

After the "remodeling job," 1929 and its ill-fated aftermath
were tagged an historical accident; it was a low-probability event,
unlikely to ever happen again ... and we drank the Kool-Aid.

No more snares! Oh, of course, it took awhile, several decades of increasing prosperity without any economic slump even remotely resembling the Great Depression, before we finally swallowed the last of that drink—and the real party was set to begin. It was in full swing until late 2007, when another series of errors, which we all thought would never happen again … did.

THE SYSTEM UNRAVELS … ONCE AGAIN

During 2008, in a matter of months, a system that had delivered increasing prosperity, year after year for more than half a century, unraveled as bankers, business leaders, hedge fund managers, politicians, and academics along with ordinary people, looked on in shocked horror in probably the most public display of how "little we know." Once again, our system was set in fault-finding mode and the blame game began. Reputations were stripped from many of the leading businesspeople, while others were shuffled off to prison. The high priest of finance himself made a very public and embarrassing mea culpa, saying he had found a flaw in the free-market ideology which guided his thinking. No more "Mr. Maestro," Alan Greenspan had made a grave mistake in keeping interest rates too low, for too long, laying the groundwork for our great housing "bubble." This bubble, much like the one in the 1920s stock market, had been fueled by allowing people without the proper resources to sustain a down phase in the investment cycle to purchase assets on paper-thin margins. While housing prices remained above the clouds, it underpinned all kinds of other spending that normally wouldn't have occurred. That spending sent a misleading signal to businesspeople to expand, so as to accommodate the *artificial* demand—overloading consumer, financial, and home-building sectors with excessive capacity that now would have to be eliminated.

Belatedly, we realized that we should not have dismantled the financial apparatus put in place during the 1930s, nor given commercial and investment banks a green light to jack up leverage to levels that would have made investment firms of the late 1920s blush. Furthermore, it was rather naïve to have encouraged our financial watchdogs to go on a "light-touch" holiday while the financial community was acting like a gang of reckless teenagers—offering no-money-down subprime mortgages and writing complex and difficult-to-understand derivatives. And, of course, in hindsight, letting Lehman go under was seen, by many, as the government's prime mistake.

If only Alan Greenspan had moved earlier to raise rates and quell the bubble, or taxpayers had come to Lehman's rescue, or regulators had tightened standards and put a halt to all that financial foolishness, we might have had a different, and happier, outcome.

Not so!

If our economy and stock market are really parts of a complex adaptive system, and I think they are, the Monday morning financial critics got it wrong. The errors were not man-made. They were of the kind that living systems, operating via a trial-and-error process, typically make. Therefore, they could not, in an ordinary sense, be man-fixed. Moreover, those errors were based on the prevailing knowledge of that time, and, on that note, they were probably legitimate errors; most anybody who had been in a position of authority would have made them.

The culprit this time, as in the 1920s, was an inappropriate appreciation of risk—a wealth-creating system populated with agents who assumed that, for all practical purposes, we had dispensed with economic and financial danger. Once a society loses sight of the fact that our world, in many respects, contains a certain amount of danger, it grants agents permission to engage in excessive and inappropriate behavior that in a system, not so blinded to risk would indeed be considered excessively "risky."

The Fatal Error

The real error made, was in *not* allowing for error. The resiliency of a system lies in its ability to absorb mistakes—and that means building in a healthy margin of safety, a reservoir of savings. But once the agents became engulfed in the perception that risk barely existed, the system adjusted to that condition by eating into its reservoir of savings. Individuals, business firms, institutions, and public entities such as state and city governments increased their purchases, narrowing the gap between their spending and income. And many went much further, spending more than their earnings. Our wealth-generating machine lowered its margin of safety drastically, leaving little room for anything to go wrong. Even small errors could no longer be tolerated. That particular sand castle had become too high.

The more complex a system becomes, the greater the number of errors. Bubble time is also peak complexity time. The particular error doesn't matter so much, as all roads lead to system failure. Much like Hercules in his battle with the nine-headed serpent Hydra, when Hercules cut off one head, two more would sprout; if we fixed one error, the problem shifted and another and more potent accident soon popped up.

The system was, in fact, corroding while its energy was seeping out. Thus, it was only a matter of time before that last grain of sand, the dreaded error—perhaps, Lehman—did us in. Actually the sorry fact is we truly needed that error in order to cleanse a rotting system—filled with too many marginal businesses of little productive merit—and discipline tipsy agents who had been driving way above the speed limit.

The bright and highly paid business and economic leaders of the past decade were drawn into a vortex of belief within an economic milieu that, in truth, should have been unbelievable. They had an ample amount of the wisdom of their period; they had risen to their pinnacles precisely because they had incorporated the accepted wisdom of their time. And as we have already seen, it's hard, very hard, to avoid being sucked into this seductive new belief; it's harder yet for the few who did avoid being drawn in to attain positions of prominence, so there are no what-ifs. Nonbelievers simply didn't have the legitimacy to differentiate themselves from the usual crackpots, who are always out there, criticizing an establishment.

AN IRON LAW OF LIVING SYSTEMS

Looking at our economic and financial world through a Newtonian lens—assigning blame and searching out causes and errors for the problems which we think can be fixed, as we would a broken pipe, to avoid a replay—misses the point. (Yet it is necessary to play out this fault-finding and error-correcting drama, as it allows a public catharsis and lays the groundwork for a restoration of faith—but in no way does it guarantee preventing a repeat of those human mistakes in some form or another.)

Something else is going on. It appears there is a little noted, but quite important, "iron law of living systems," which can best be understood by viewing this system through a Darwinian lens. And we best pay attention, as we, in our social life, are governed by it.

The behavior of human agents as a group is quite predictable. To repeat, it is, for the most part, an adaptive response to some important change in its co-evolving external environment; this is a shift powerful enough to provoke a lesson of pain or pleasure that resonates throughout the agent part of the living system. Quite simply, a long-lasting period of wealth destruction will provide a lesson of pain that induces agents to adopt a cautious, risk-avoiding behavioral pattern. On the reverse side of the coin, a period of sustained and robust economic expansion will send out an unmistakable message of pleasure that flips the prior behavioral pattern to an "animal-spirited" risk-taking one. There is nothing new here: just agents responding to a change in their external environment.

Now for the "paradox": After enough time so that most agents have joined in a risk-avoiding behavioral response, caution graduates through fear to "brace for the worst," and we will experience exactly the opposite of what that fear-ridden agent public had expected: a robust and sustained business expansion will surprise them. And similarly, after a risk-taking behavioral pattern has had a long enough run so that "animal spirits" have been upgraded to excessive greed, and financial margins of safety have become razor thin, the economy will deliver a painful period of chilling wealth destruction, the very opposite of what overly optimistic agents had been looking for.

There is an important interaction between the behavioral patterns of agents and the external environment, in our case the economy, and each eventually pulls the rug out from beneath the other. A long period of rapid economic growth is predicated on a reservoir of agent caution. That caution will motivate agents to keep an extra-large financial margin of safety—a huge pile of savings—which will allow the system to deflect errors and, thus, build immunity against further wealth destruction into the system.

During this long period of growing economic prosperity, risk-avoiding behavior slowly turns into "animal-spirited" behavior. But as long as the cautious crowd's reservoir of savings remains above a safe level, it is able to keep "animal spirits" from gaining free rein and economic outcomes of robust economic growth will, for the most part, still reflect this cautious behavioral restraint. Yet, human agents only see outcomes and adopt behavioral patterns to reflect those observations. They do not factor in that the abandoned behavioral mode was responsible for those outcomes. So they will continue to respond to the prior favorable outcomes by crowding into a risk-taking behavioral mode until the remaining cautious crowd is unable to deflect their rambunctious behavior. A mammoth horde of risk takers, looking for decent yields, will venture into riskier and riskier areas of the economy and the stock market until they have pulled the carpet out from beneath their very own feet, sabotaging the sustainable period of good economic times they had been expecting … and oops, another historical accident occurs.

The "paradox" is that the external environment also responds—becoming unexpectedly fragile or robust—to the changes in agent behavior: this is an iron law of living systems. Yes, system doctors may be able to extend the good (up) phase and tame the bad (down) phase, or perhaps delay crossing over into "bubble" territory, but, try as we may, that might be the best we can do without taking away the freedom for the agents to make an adaptive response.

Risk Is Not What It Seems

In reality, risk it is at its highest when nearly everyone thinks it is absent; when most people see it as great, it is actually quite low. It is part of the great secret that author Nikos Kazantzakis had Sly Thomas reveal in his book *The Last Temptation of Christ*, which reads, "A prophet is one who, when everyone else despairs, hopes. And when everyone else hopes, he despairs. You'll ask why. It's because he has mastered the great secret: The Wheel Turns."[5]

Need we bore you with a repeat of all those highly expected events, outlined earlier in the book, which never came to fruition? The infectious optimism that pervaded throughout the country preceding the depression of the 1930s; the late 1940s hand-wringing about a widely predicted postwar depression which never happened; the dismal outlook of the late 1970s when the nation was beset by worsening energy shortages, business stagnation, and galloping inflation, just before a great resurgence of economic vitality was to begin; and, finally, the public euphoria in the years before the last bubble burst in late 2007. None of these worries or optimistic promises, which so rattled or electrified the American public for years, ever materialized.

Every so often a trend has a second phase: a bubble in a bull trend that takes us on a roller-coaster ride that ends badly. It flips into a bear market, which unlike most receding markets falls into a dark hole, which becomes the second phase of a bear market, wherein there is a huge destruction of wealth. While the system bumps along the bottom, well below former highs, for a long, long time, human agents "stumble around in the dark." And these bubble-flips will be the undoing of many a "Jeremy Siegel"–buy-and-hold stock market investor.

WE ARE VICTIMS OF THE PARADOX

We live in a Darwinian world, which is filled with nasty surprises, errors, paradoxes, meaningless chatter, and most of all, unsettling change—discontinuity. It is a world wherein most people need some rationale or belief system in order to point them in the direction of either pursuing opportunity or avoiding danger. Yet these beliefs, while providing people with the courage to select the proper form of behavior, also carry a disclaimer in the fine print, unseen to the human eye, which is when too many others also believe, all guarantees as to the viability of that belief are off.

We become victims of the "paradox." That's because human behavior adapts to the shifts in the external environment, but in so doing removes the behavioral premise that the environment was based on. This happens in bubbles, as we saw, and again when the market slips into a dark hole. It also occurs during one-phase trends, only in those cases the bubble like symptoms are considerably milder; they are not societywide events.

If we hope to avoid becoming victims, the trick is to come up with our own personal search engine that is able to identify the *critical levels* that indicate a change in trend (a phase transition). In the next chapter, I will present an algorithm that has done a "good enough" job in identifying those important tipping points.

PART 4

SELECTING ASSET CLASS "FITS"

The second important concept borrowed from Darwinian biology is "selection," in our case selecting a risk asset class only when it "fits" the investment landscape. We designed a search engine (an algorithm) to pinpoint the "critical levels" that play an important role in complex adaptive systems. It then tells us whether or not the "risk" asset class is a good fit with the prevailing investment climate. If so, we select it; if not, we select either the intermediate or the long-term Treasury.

CHAPTER 9

CRITICAL LEVELS IN THE STOCK MARKET

Active investing is a tricky business. We are dealing with a future that we cannot see very well. That brings us to the complex adaptive systems concept of *critical levels*, mentioned earlier in the book. In the stock market, these levels usually indicate a phase transition, from a bull to bear trend, and vice versa. Now I am going to introduce a simple algorithm that acts as a search engine to identify those important levels, wherein a new trend is birthed.

I will use what stock market technicians call the *channel breakout* method, tracking closing prices only. A channel breakout occurs when each and every closing price within the channel (which can be a given number of days, weeks, or even months) is breached. Suppose we are talking about a 50-day channel. The first close above *all* the prior 50-days' settling prices signals an upside breakout, indicating a bullish trend is in process (see Figure 9-1). According to this strategy, it remains in effect until a closing price below each and every one of the prior 50 end-of-the-day prices is recorded. This downside channel breakout alerts followers that the trend has now turned from bull to bear, and it continues in force until another bullish breakout takes place. While this algorithm does not attempt to pick tops or bottoms, it does allow investors to climb on board, "adapting" early on in a new trend.

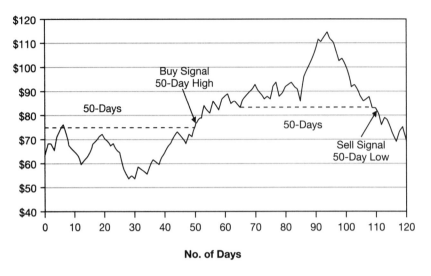

Figure 9-1 50-Day Channel Breakout.

As I said, the algorithm is going to be a simple method. That means avoiding any hint of *data mining*, which refers to parsing the data with a fine-tooth comb until you discover some obscure pattern that is probably random and, most likely, will prove meaningless.

One year is, without a doubt, the most prevalent longer-term unit of time that businesses, governments, and people use to measure things because it includes all four seasons, a full set of holidays with their special-buying customs, and school-year vacation habits. Businesses issue annual reports, which highlight yearly earnings. Taxes are paid at annual intervals. Governments figure their budgets on a yearly basis. Individuals and nations celebrate birthdays once a year. I will align our algorithm with the habits of society and select 1 year (365 days) as the parameter for the downside channel. Any close below that level will indicate we are in a bearish trend.

However, because of a widely acknowledged bias to the upside, an inbred "growth gene," so to speak, in both our economy and stock market, it makes sense to set the channel needed for a bullish breakout at a lesser amount. The American economy, since it joined in the Industrial Revolution, has grown at an inflation-adjusted rate of approximately 3.5 percent per year. Our stock market, which is tethered to economic activity, has delivered a compounded annual return of about 9.87 percent since 1926. Moreover, monetary and government authorities stand at the ready to do what they can to force-feed the economy to keep businesses humming.

The easiest and simplest solution in selecting this channel, again avoiding any hint of data mining, is to cut the year in half and use an even 6 months as the time frame that must be breached on the upside before an all clear buy signal is given.

Three more decisions are necessary before we test this strategy. First we must decide what time period to use to examine the results. This period is important as it is quite easy to select some particularly favorable time span and parade it around as a representative sample. In this case we begin with 1926, which has become the industry gold standard as to the beginning of reliable stock market data.

Next, we need to decide which stock index should be used to time our buying and selling. Currently the S&P 500 Index, which accounts for approximately 75 percent of total market capitalization, is the most widely used by investment professionals. However, it was not set up in its present form until 1957. Before that time (actually before the beginning of 1958, which allows for an accumulation of some data to take measurements) we will use the Dow Jones Industrial Average (DJIA), which was the most popular index in the earlier part of the last century (in fact, most media, both print and broadcast, are still fixated on the Dow).

The third decision we need to make is what to do with cash when it is not invested in stocks. We should purchase intermediate (5-year) government notes. As we saw earlier, they provided an extra 1.73 percent of return above riskless 90-day T-Bills, with a minuscule amount of risk (i.e., average underperformance) during the last 85 years.

CRITICAL LEVEL–SEARCH METHOD: BUY AND SELL

I will call this critical level–search method, Buy and Sell (B&S), and to test it, we will use the Dow Jones Industrial Average until 1958, and then switch to the S&P 500 for the remainder of the period. To repeat: A 6-month channel breakout on the upside provides a buy signal, which remains in effect until a 1-year channel is breached on the downside. This breach becomes the telltale sell sign (dump equities and buy 5-year Treasuries), which also will remain in force until a new buy signal is given.

As the DJIA was clearly in an uptrend on December 31, 1925 (see Figure 9-2), we initiated our test with a purchase on the close of that day at 156.66.

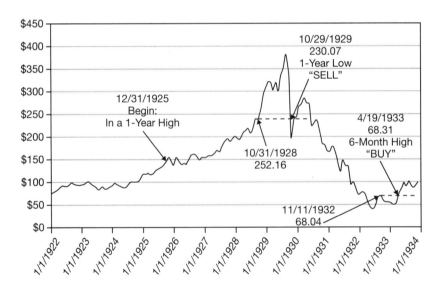

Figure 9-2   Dow Jones Industrial Average (DJIA), 1922–1933.

The stock market remained in that bull trend for another 3 ³/₄ years, or until October 29, 1929. On that date, the Dow closed at 230.07, breaching the lowest low of the prior 1-year channel, which had occurred on October 31, 1928, at 252.16, as seen in Figure 9-1. It was B&S's first sell signal and it earned its spurs by protecting investors from an additional 82 percent decline before the bottom was reached in early July 1932, at the hard-to-fathom low level of 41.22. A heads-up signal to purchase stocks was not given until the end of the day on April 19, 1933, when the DJIA exceeded the highest close of its prior 6-month channel, which had been set at 68.04 on November 11, 1932. By the way, for those of you keeping score, that April 1933 purchase at 68.31 was 70.31 percent below B&S's October 1929 sale. Meanwhile, during that time, if B&S followers had invested in 5-year government Treasuries, they would have increased their net wealth by 12.68 percent since the sell date.

Table 9-1 shows the history of all B&S's purchases and sales from the very end of 1925 through the last day of 2010 and the returns generated. Dividend income was added based on the yield reported in Standard & Poor's "Security Price Index Record."

Table 9-1   Buy and Sell Signals: 1926–2010

	BUY	DJIA	SELL	DJIA	DIV*	ADJ SELL	% PROFIT/ LOSS
1.	12/31/25	156.66	10/29/29	230.07	40.13	270.20	+72.48
2.	04/19/33	68.31	09/07/37	164.39	26.27	190.66	179.93
3.	06/29/38	135.87	05/14/40	128.27	13.36	141.63	4.24
4.	07/21/41	129.51	11/28/41	114.66	3.20	117.86	(9.00)
5.	09/24/42	109.11	09/09/46	172.03	29.15	201.18	84.38
6.	07/11/47	184.77	05/31/49	168.36	20.53	188.89	2.23
7.	08/05/49	179.07	06/16/53	262.88	61.05	323.93	80.90
8.	11/05/53	279.09	02/11/57	457.44	58.19	515.63	84.75
9.	05/13/57	502.21	10/07/57	452.42	7.62	460.04	(8.40)
	S&P			**S&P**			
10.			10/07/57	42.22			
11.	04/18/58	42.71	02/16/60	54.73	3.14	57.87	+35.39
12.	08/24/60	58.07	09/26/60	53.06	0.17	53.23	(8.33)

Table 9-1   Buy and Sell Signals: 1926–2010 (Continued)

	BUY	S&P	SELL	S&P	DIV*	ADJ SELL†	% PROFIT/ (LOSS)
13.	12/30/60	58.11	05/09/62	64.26	2.82	67.08	15.24
14.	11/23/62	61.54	07/27/66	83.60	9.37	92.97	48.36
15.	01/20/67	86.07	03/04/68	87.92	3.34	91.26	5.75
16.	04/17/68	96.81	06/23/69	96.23	3.63	99.86	3.01
17.	11/30/70	87.20	05/14/73	105.90	7.64	113.54	30.71
18.	02/12/75	79.92	03/30/77	98.54	8.33	106.87	34.25
18.	04/26/78	96.82	08/31/81	122.79	19.54	142.33	51.24
20.	08/31/82	119.51	05/22/84	153.88	12.19	166.07	39.25
21.	08/03/84	162.35	10/19/87	224.84	26.10	250.94	56.88
22.	06/14/88	274.30	08/21/90	321.86	23.76	345.62	26.59
23.	02/04/91	348.34	11/22/00	1322.36	140.90	1463.26	371.30
24.	05/12/03	945.11	01/16/08	1373.20	107.42	1480.62	58.14
25.	06/01/09	942.87	12/31/10	1257.64‡	33.83	1291.47	36.97
Average profit	55.24%						

Key:
* Dividends
† Adjusted sell price; includes dividend price plus dividends received
‡ Still in process

How well did these signals perform? Only 24 buy signals, including the present one, which has not yet been completed, were given during this whole 85-year period. Of the 23 concluded buys, 20, or 87 percent, were closed out at a profit and 15 trades measured 25 percent or more (including two that reached into triple digits). Only three purchases ended with a loss to investors; the largest from *point of entry*, when a purchase was first made, was 9 percent, which followed the buy of July 1941. Three others, the buys in 1938, 1947, and 1968, were rescued by dividend income, which provided them with a small net plus. All told, the average return on those 23 buys plus the uncompleted 24th buy was 55.24 percent.

However, only seven of the sell signals provided B&S investors with a chance to repurchase stocks at a level cheaper (after adjusting for dividends received) than when sold. Following another three sell signals, the return from intermediate Treasuries enabled B&S investors to outperform the B&H strategy, which had only eked out a small profit by the time the next buy signal came. That brings B&S to 10 outperformances, or 43 percent of the 23 sell signals.

Protection from Peril

A 43 percent success ratio on the sell signals may not sound like much, but it doesn't tell the whole story. Keep in mind, search engines are not magical. As we saw in evolution, they operate with a great deal of error. The object of the sell signals is to protect investors from peril and the B&S method does so by pinpointing gathering storms. However, as we all know, not all storms brewing at sea build into deadly hurricanes. So too with potential stock market dangers; many do not snowball into real danger. All and all, a better than 40 percent success ratio for an algorithm attempting to select the proper critical sell level, in an uncertain game such as investing, is a "good-enough" outcome.

The B&S strategy's most attractive feature was its ability to protect followers from the four bone-chilling paper losses B&H investors suffered following sell alerts in 1929, 1973, 2000, and 2008 (see Table 9-2). In all four cases, B&H participants saw the value of their stock portfolio decline by more than 20 percent before an all clear B&S buy signal was given.

Table 9-2   "Out-of-Market" Periods: S&P Performance versus 5-year Government Bond

SELLS	DJIA	REBUY	DJIA	P/L*	NAV 1000	5-YEAR TREAS.	NAV 1000	B&S: OVER/ UNDER PERF†
1. 10/29/29	230.07	04/19/33	68.31	(50.89)	491	12.68%	1127	+63.57%
2. 09/07/37	164.39	06/29/38	135.87	(9.58)	444	2.30	1153	11.88
3. 05/14/40	128.37	07/21/41	129.51	2.38	455	1.13	1166	(1.25)

Table 9-2   "Out-of-Market" Periods: S&P Performance versus 5-year Government Bond *(Continued)*

SELLS	DJIA	REBUY	REBUY	P/L*	NAV 1000	5-YEAR TREAS.	NAV 1000	B&S: OVER/ UNDER PERF†
4. 11/28/41	114.66	09/24/42	109.11	1.36	461	(1.40)	1149	(2.76)
5. 09/09/46	172.03	07/11/47	184.77	11.66	515	0.88	1160	(10.78)
6. 05/31/49	168.36	08/05/49	179.07	7.63	554	1.10	1172	(6.53)
7. 06/16/53	262.88	11/05/53	279.09	7.06	593	3.45	1213	(3.61)
8. 02/11/57	457.44	05/13/57	502.21	10.79	657	(0.53)	1296	(11.32)
	S&P		**S&P**					
9. 10/07/57	42.22	04/18/58	42.71	+3.36	679	+9.11	1316	+5.75
10. 02/16/60	54.73	08/24/60	58.07	7.93	733	7.21	1411	(0.72)
11. 09/26/60	53.06	12/30/60	58.11	10.48	810	1.34	1430	(9.14)
12. 05/09/62	64.26	11/23/62	61.54	(2.47)	790	1.95	1458	4.45
13. 07/27/66	83.60	01/20/67	86.07	4.64	826	4.51	1524	(0.13)
14. 03/04/68	87.92	04/17/68	96.81	10.53	913	0.33	1529	(10.20)
15. 06/23/69	96.23	11/30/70	87.20	(4.42)	873	8.17	1654	12.59
16. 05/14/73	105.90	02/12/75	79.92	(22.18)	679	11.88	1850	34.06
17. 03/30/77	98.54	04/26/78	96.82	3.34	702	4.13	1926	0.77
18. 08/31/81	122.79	08/31/82	119.51	+2.91	722	+27.67	2459	+24.76
19. 05/22/84	153.88	08/03/84	162.35	6.44	768	5.17	2587	(1.27)
20. 10/19/87	224.84	06/14/88	274.30	23.94	952	11.57	2886	(12.37)
21. 08/21/90	321.86	02/04/91	348.34	9.95	1047	8.28	3125	(1.67)
22. 12/22/00	1322.16	05/13/03	945.11	(5.51)	780	27.75	3992	53.18
23. 01/16/08	1373.20	06/01/09	942.87	(28.76)	556	4.54	4173	33.30

CMPD Return   = S&P (2.81)%

5-year Treasury   = 7.19%

Total "Out-of-Market" Years = 20.57

* Includes dividend income

† Difference between 5-year Treasuries and stock performance during "out-of-market" periods

Source: Banking and Monetary Statistics, 1914– 1941, 1941–1970; T. Coleman, L. Fisher, and R. Ibbotson, *Historical U.S. Treasury Yield Curve,* 1993 edition.

Meanwhile, unbloodied B&S investors, sitting in intermediate government bonds were reaping positive returns, from 4.54 percent to 27.67 percent, and in each of those cases, B&S outperformed B&H by more than 33 percent. It was this "dodge the big loss" feature that provided the B&S method with its superb risk-control trait.

All told, during the 20.57 years when B&S investors were out of the stock market and tucked safely into intermediate Treasuries, they enjoyed a compounded 7.19 percent return on that investment; meanwhile B&H investors watched the value of their investments, even after accounting for dividends, dwindle at a compounded (2.81) percent rate. See Table 9–2. An investor specializing in buying equities only at the precise time that B&S registered a sell signal, and who exited the trade with perfect pitch on the subsequent buy signal, would have lost 44.4 percent after participating in all 23 trades. On the other hand, an investor choosing those same dates to buy and sell 5-year government notes would have racked up a 317.3 percent profit by period's end. Some difference!

A good example of dodging a big, bad bear market was B&S's last sell signal given on January 16, 2008, as shown in Table 9-2, with the S&P 500 at 1373.20, just a bit more than 12 percent off its all-time high. Those who sold at that point would have avoided a further 50 percent falloff before prices bottomed at 676.53 in early March 2009. And had they collected Treasury note interest while watching from the sidelines and repurchased on the June 1, 2009, buy signal at 942.87, their net loss from the 2007 top at 1565.15 would have been just 8.26 percent, a loss of 12.26 percent from the stock market peak to the sell signal followed by a 4.54 percent profit in 5-year notes, as opposed to a paper loss of almost 40 percent for buy-and-hold investors on that date. See Tables 9-1 and 9-2.

Annual Returns

Now we are going to translate the B&S strategy's record into annual returns and examine how well it stacked up against the B&H stock market program. See Table 9-3.

Table 9-3   Buy and Sell : Annual Returns

YEAR ($1000)	B&S RETURN	NAV 1000	POTHOLE PAIN <20%>	B&H RETURN	NAV 1000	POTHOLE PAIN <20%>
1926	+11.62	1116		+11.62	1116	
1927	37.49	1535		37.49	1535	
1928	43.61	2204		43.61	2204	
1929	(17.96)	1808		(8.42)	2018	
1930	6.72	1930		(24.90)	1515	
1931	(2.32)	1885		(43.34)	858	
1932	8.81	2051		(8.19)	788	(64.21)
1933	47.39	3023		53.99	1214	
1934	(1.44)	2979		(1.44)	1196	
1935	47.67	4400		47.67	1766	
1936	33.92	5992		33.92	2366	
1937	(3.76)	5670		(35.03)	1537	(35.03)
1938	14.85	6512		31.12	2015	
1939	(0.41)	6486		(0.41)	2007	
1940	(11.92)	5713		(9.78)	1810	
1941	(9.14)	5190	(20.30)	(11.59)	1600	(20.54)
1942	10.05	5712		20.34	1927	
1943	25.90	7191		25.90	2426	
1944	19.75	8612		19.75	2905	
1945	36.44	11,750		36.44	3963	
1946	(7.70)	10,845		(8.07)	3643	
1947	1.14	10,969		5.71	3851	
1948	5.50	11,572		5.50	4063	
1949	13.46	13,130		18.79	4827	
1950	31.71	17,293		31.71	6357	
1951	24.02	21,447		24.02	7884	
1952	18.37	25,387		18.37	9333	
1953	(2.84)	24,666		(0.99)	9240	
1954	52.62	37,648		52.62	14,102	

Table 9-3   Buy and Sell: Annual Returns *(Continued)*

YEAR	B&S RETURN	NAV	POTHOLE PAIN <20%>	B&H RETURN	NAV	POTHOLE PAIN <20%>
1955	31.56	49,626		31.56	18,553	
1956	6.56	52,775		6.56	19,770	
1957	(11.76)	46,568		(10.78)	17,639	
1958	36.99	63,794		43.36	25,287	
1959	11.96	71,424		11.96	28,312	
1960	(8.84)	65,110		0.47	28,445	
1961	26.89	82,618		26.89	36,093	
1962	(4.75)	78,693		(8.73)	32,943	
1963	22.80	96,636		22.80	40,453	
1964	16.48	112,561		16.48	47,120	
1965	12.45	126,575		12.45	52,987	
1966	(4.25)	121,196		(10.06)	47,657	
1967	16.15	140,769		23.98	59,085	
1968	0.70	141,754		11.06	65,620	
1969	(9.50)	128,287		(8.50)	60,042	
1970	19.19	152,906		3.86	62,360	
1971	14.30	174,771		14.30	71,277	

YEAR	B&S RETURN	NAV	NAV–2 1000	POTHOLE PAIN <20%>	B&H RETURN	NAV	POTHOLE PAIN <20%>
1972	18.99	207,960	1190		18.99	84,813	
1973	(5.44)	196,647	1125		(14.69)	72,379	
1974	5.69	207,836	1189		(26.47)	53,221	**(37.25)**
1975	18.66	246,619	1411		37.23	73,035	
1976	23.93	305,635	1749		23.93	90,512	
1977	(4.47)	291,973	1671		(7.16)	84,313	
1978	3.85	303,214	1735		6.57	89,544	
1979	18.61	359,642	2058		18.61	106,202	
1980	32.50	476,525	2727		32.50	140,726	
1981	5.29	501,733	2871		(4.92)	133,802	

Table 9-3   Buy and Sell: Annual Returns *(Continued)*

YEAR	B&S RETURN	NAV	NAV–2	POTHOLE PAIN <20%>	B&H RETURN	NAV	POTHOLE PAIN <20%>
1982	35.75	681,123	3897		21.55	162,637	
1983	22.56	834,760	4776		22.56	199,323	
1984	4.77	874,578	5004		6.27	211,825	
1985	31.73	1,152,082	6592		31.73	279,038	
1986	18.67	1,367,175	7823		18.67	331,134	
1987	2.63	1,403,132	8028		5.25	348,519	
1988	7.34	1,506,122	8618		16.61	406,407	
1989	31.69	1,983,412	11,384		31.69	535,198	
1990	(0.82)	1,967,148	11,256		(3.10)	518,697	
1991	24.99	2,458,738	14,068		30.47	676,744	
1992	7.62	2,646,094	15,140		7.62	728,312	
1993	10.08	2,912,821	16,666		10.08	801,726	
1994	1.32	2,951,270	16,886		1.32	812,308	
1995	37.58	4,060,357	23,232		37.58	1,117,574	
1996	22.96	4,992,615	28,567		22.96	1,374,169	
1997	33.36	6,658,151	38,096		33.36	1,832,592	
1998	28.58	8,561,051	48,984		28.58	2,356,347	
1999	21.04	10,362,296	59,291		21.04	2,852,122	
2000	(6.09)	9,731,232	55,680		(9.10)	2,592,579	
2001	7.62	10,472752	59,923		(11.89)	2,284,321	
2002	12.93	11,826125	67,671		(22.10)	1,779,486	**(37.61)**
2003	21.12	14,324716	81,963		28.68	2,289,843	
2004	10.88	15,883,245	90,880		10.88	2,538,978	
2005	4.91	16,663,112	95,342		4.91	2,663,641	
2006	15.79	19,294,217	110,397		15.79	3,084,230	
2007	5.49	20,353,470	116,458		5.49	3,253,555	
2008	1.57	20,673,019	118,286		(37.00)	2,049,739	**(37.00)**
2009	15.24	23,823,587	13,6313		26.46	2,592,100	
2010	15.06	27,411,419	156842		15.06	2,982,470	

Table 9-3   Buy and Sell: Annual Returns *(Continued)*

	1926–2010		1972–2010			
	B&S	B&H	B&S	B&H	SB 60/40	INT. GOV
CMPD Return	+12.77%	+9.87%	+13.84%	+10.05%	+9.60%	+7.79%
90-Day T-Bill (Less)	+3.62%	+3.62%	+5.56%	+5.56%	+5.56%	+5.56%
Excess Return	+9.15%	+6.25%	+8.28%	+4.49%	+4.04%	+2.23%

	1926–2010		1972–2010			
RISK MEASURES	B&S	B&H	B&S	B&H	SB 60/40	INT. GOV.
Standard Deviation	15.58	20.39	12.11	18.33	11.54	6.51
Avg. Underperformance	(2.09)	(4.98)	(1.71)	(5.10)	(2.94)	(1.42)
Gain-to-Pain Ratio	4.38	1.26	4.84	0.88	1.37	1.57
Worst Drawdown	(20.30)	(64.21)	(6.09)	(37.61)	(38.44)	(5.14)
2nd Worst Drawdown	(17.96)	(37.61)	(5.44)	(37.25)	(20.39)	(2.40)
No. of Yrs. Outperformed T-Bill	55	55	28	26	26	23

When B&S was invested in the stock market throughout the whole year, we used *Ibbotson's* annual figures. Partial year returns were calculated from the appropriate indexes with dividends added. Interest income and capital gains, from intermediate government bonds, when out of the stock market were also added (Federal Reserve "Historical Statistical Data" and *Ibbotson's* figures).

The results speak for themselves. Over the whole 85-year period, B&S's compounded annual return came in at 12.77 percent, which was 2.90 percent better than B&H's 9.87 percent figure (see Table 9-3). Although this might not seem like all that much to beat the drums about, when tabulated over the whole 1926 to 2010 period, it was enough to deliver a more than nine times greater total return. A $1000 B&H investment would have grown to an impressive $2,982,470 by period's end, while the same initial investment in B&S would have sprouted into a mouthwatering $27,411,419 nest egg by the year-end 2010.

A Lower Risk Profile

Yet, the really *outstanding feature* of the B&S method was its far lower risk profile. The B&H strategy had a standard deviation of 20.39, while the B&S method weighed in at 15.58—or about 23.6 percent lower. But for the entire 1926–2010 period, B&S's average underperformance came in at 2.09 percent (total underperformance of 177.76 divided by 85 observed years), and that was only about 42 percent of B&H's AU of 4.98. It would be fair to say that, by the measure of average underperformance, B&S was about 58 percent less risky than B&H. That difference is quite impressive, certainly more so than its 24 percent lower standard deviation. Also, B&S spewed out an excess return ER of 4.38 percent for each 1 percent of risk, which trounced B&H's gain-to-pain (G/P) ratio of 1.26. However, B&S beat a risk-free investment in 55 of the 85 years, the same as B&H.

Moreover, B&S fell into only one deep (greater than 20 percent) pothole along its way, which produced only 0.30 percent of torture. The year 1929 also came fairly close (at 17.96 percent), but held the 20 percent barrier.

Figures for the 1972–2010 period were just as impressive. B&S's annualized return won out 13.84 percent to 10.05 percent, and its total dollar return was nearly four times that of B&H's. Average underperformance of just (1.71) was 34 percent of a passive S&P's, indicating it was 66 percent less risky. And of course its G/P ratio of 4.84 left B&H's G/P ratio of 0.88 in the dust.

To Buy-and-Sell Critics-to-Be

Before we can declare case closed, I realize some critics will bemoan the additional trading, 23 sells and repurchases, which would have resulted in increased *transaction costs* (commissions plus price slippage at execution) along with the additional capital gains taxes paid. Yes, but keep in mind stocks are often held in IRAs or 401(k)'s, which are not taxed until a distribution is made, usually many years in the future. Also, come on now; 23 sells and 24 purchases, over an 85-year span—about one round turn every 3½ years—doesn't amount to a heck of a lot of actual trading. Additionally, some of B&S's actual profits were understated as, unlike *Ibbotson*, we did not account for the reinvestment of dividends during years wherein we reentered the stock market.

The B&S strategy also outperformed SB60/40 hands down during the 85-year period, racking up a 4.24 percent compounded return advantage, which provided investors with nearly a 25-fold increase in total return. And it did so with an average underperformance that was about 25 percent lower, even though its standard deviation was approximately 25 percent higher. Additionally, its gain-to-pain ratio clocked in at almost two and a half times the SB60/40 number.

Moreover, B&S's defensive qualities can be a great advantage to be used as a tool to develop all sorts of innovative techniques to gain further strategic advantages. One possibility would be to use more aggressive investment vehicles, such as high beta or momentum-type stocks during market uptrends—and, at times, even some leverage.

BUY & SELL WRAP-UP

I introduced B&S as a simple trend-following method, which, over an 85-year time span, did a pretty good job of identifying the critical levels, wherein bull and bear trends took on a life of their own. While not perfect, it was good enough to beat a sit-on-your-hands-do-nothing passive approach in an uncertain and pothole-filled investment world. It would have guided investors to their investment goals with both more gain and considerably less pain, while sidestepping much of the economic noise that confuses most investors.

To sum up:

- A simple trend-spotting method, such as B&S, designed to "avoid the big loss" has a superb risk-control mechanism built into its architecture.
- B&S was more profitable than both B&H and SB60/40, while also sporting a lower average underperformance than both. And by protecting investors from giant-sized losses, B&S opened the door for the use of more volatile investment vehicles, which promise even greater upside returns.

Although every so often, this 1-year/6-month algorithm, based on rhythms of agent behavior, screws up (errors, you remember), it has been enormously successful spotting turns in the stock market for 85 years.

Now we will turn our attention to the prime financial system assets—gold and long-term Treasuries—and see if the same algorithm that allowed us to beat a passive stock market strategy will also enable us to outfox a simple gold and Treasury passive strategy.

CHAPTER 10

GOLD AND LONG-TERM TREASURIES: BUY AND REPLACE

Gold may be the best barometer as to whether the general price level is on, or soon to be on, a rising or falling trend. When prices are increasing to a point which threatens a bout of inflation or if there is even a hint that the pace of price increases is about to quicken—for example, the Fed has flooded the banking system with liquidity or excessive government borrowing has undermined faith in the nation's paper currency (indicating inflation problems down the road)—gold will usually deliver returns far superior to equities, as witnessed in periods from 1972 to 1980 and from 2003 to 2010. However, when our monetary authorities have a firm grip on the nation's money and credit reins, constraining inflationary potential, as they did from 1981 until 2003, gold is likely to be an awful investment.

Yet when gold is bleeping out an "inflation all-clear" signal, we can usually count on long-term Treasuries to spring to life, as lenders feel quite comfortable tying their money up for an extended period. At the same time, the Fed is able to help support economic growth via nudging interest rates lower. Interest rates, especially if they are not already at historically low rates, typically fall and 20-year Treasuries deliver generous returns.

This reciprocal relationship between gold and long-term Treasuries, wherein one typically ebbs when the other flows, is one of, if not the most reliable investment relationships in the investment world. As we recall from earlier in the book, a passive gold and long-term Treasury portfolio split 50/50 G/T would have returned a compounded 9.96 percent with an average under-performance of (3.39) during the "39 years" ending in 2010, also shown in Table 10-2. In this chapter, I am going to present an active gold/long-term Treasury strategy geared to beating that passive version.

BUY AND REPLACE STRATEGY

Yet, rather than including both gold and long-term Treasuries in the portfolio at the same time, I will attempt to select the one more likely to be in tune with the state of the financial system. To do so, we will use the same 1-year/6-month search engine that worked so well in the stock market to switch from one asset class to the other. In this case, we are going to focus the algo-rithm on gold, as it is the "risk" asset. Long-term bonds are the defensive seeking safety asset. Much like stocks, once gold breaches a critical price level, it changes the direction of the feedback loops, setting off a new long-term trend that takes on a life of its own.

But first, there is one important difference. While partici-pants in our overall economic and social system, agents and insti-tutions alike, are geared to promoting economic growth, that system abhors inflation. The general consensus is that inflation, and especially rapid inflation, is not good for us and we are there-fore prepared to man the barricades to prevent it from getting out of hand. While the wind is at a rising stock market's back, gold rallies run dead-smack into gusty headwinds. Quite simply, it is much harder to get a period of sustained inflation going than to get an economic expansion percolating. So while we made it eas-ier to buy stocks and harder to sell them, it makes a great deal of sense to make it harder to buy gold and easier to sell (switching to Treasuries). And the way to do so is to flip our 1 year/6-month search engine on its head, buying gold on a 1-year high in the price of London gold and switching to long-term Treasuries exiting gold when the price of gold falls to a 6-month low.

The results of this gold/Treasuries buy and replace strategy (called B&R) are presented in Table 10-1.

Table 10-1   Gold and Long-Term Treasuries: Buy and Replace

A. BASED ON LONDON CASH PM GOLD PRICE

	BUY	YIELD	SELL	YIELD	GAIN/(LOSS)%	NAV 1000
1.	12/31/71	43.625	11/14/73	90.00	106.30	2063
2.	01/17/74	128.35	05/05/75	163.50	27.39	2628
3.	02/23/77	139.20	12/10/80	579.00	315.95	10,931
4.	09/07/82	481.00	06/06/83	407.80	(15.22)	9268
5.	01/14/86	341.00	02/01/88	452.70	32.76	12,304
6.	01/12/90	416.25	04/30/90	367.75	(11.65)	10,871
7.	05/13/93	367.00	12/06/94	375.75	2.38	11,129
8.	01/05/96	395.90	06/06/96	384.85	(2.79)	10,819
9.	09/28/99	301.50	03/30/00	275.75	(8.54)	9895
10.	09/17/01	293.25	05/10/04	375.00	27.88	12,654
11.	10/25/04	429.15	10/10/06	573.30	33.59	16,904
12.	09/07/07	701.00	08/08/08	852.50	21.61	20,557
13.	09/07/09	993.00	12/31/20	1421.10*	43.11	29,419

B. BASED ON 20-YEAR TREASURY INTEREST RATE †

	BUY	YIELD	SELL	YIELD	YIELD	CHANGE IN GAIN/LOSS %	NAV 1000
1.	11/14/73	7.39	01/17/74	7.47	+0.08	+0.41%	1004
2.	05/05/75	8.26	02/23/77	7.72	(0.54)	19.97	1205
3.	12/10/80	12.85	09/07/82	12.29	(0.56)	32.58	1597
4.	06/06/83	11.06	01/14/86	9.75	(1.31)	45.19	2319
5.	02/01/88‡	8.34	01/12/90	8.14	(0.20)	17.16	2717
6.	04/30/90‡	9.02	05/13/93	6.49	(2.53)	58.98	4319
7.	12/06/94	7.93	01/05/96	6.11	(1.82)	29.76	5605

Table 10-1   Gold and Long-Term Treasuries: Buy and Replace *(Continued)*

B. BASED ON 20-YEAR TREASURY INTEREST RATE †

	BUY	YIELD	SELL	YIELD	YIELD	CHANGE IN GAIN/LOSS %	NAV
8.	06/06/96	7.08	09/28/99	6.47	(0.61)	30.12	7293
9.	03/30/00	6.26	09/17/01	5.44	(0.82)	19.00	8679
10.	05/10/04	5.54	10/25/04	4.74	(0.80)	12.62	9774
11.	10/10/06	4.96	09/07/07	4.73	(0.23)	7.42	10,499
12.	08/08/08	4.58	09/08/09†	4.24	(0.34)	6.83	11,216

	GOLD	TREASURIES	
Time invested in =	19.67 years	19.33 years	
CMPD Return =	18.76%	13.32%	Total = 16.03%

* Buy = Still in process

† =The gold signal on 09/07/09 was Labor Day in the U.S. Treasuries were sold the following day.

‡ =The 20-year government bond was discontinued at the end of 1986 and reintroduced in October 1993. During that interval I use a combined 10-year and 30-year government bond.

During the 1972–2010 period we completed 12 gold and a like amount of Treasury trades, in addition to the current gold trade. The time spent in each asset class was fairly evenly divided: approximately 19.67 years in gold and the remaining 19.33 years in Treasuries. To compute the Treasury returns during years when purchases or sales were made, we used the Fidelity "online" bond calculator.

As we can see, 8 of the 12 completed gold trades were profitable, contributing to a robust 18.76 percent compounded return during the time invested in gold. The biggest loser was (15.22) percent, on the trade initiated in September 1982. Table 10-1 also shows the level of the 20-year rate at the time all 12 long-term Treasury buys and sells were made. Following 11 of the 12 Treasury purchases, the yield was lower—meaning a higher bond price—at the time gold made a new 1-year high. The bond performance was actually more consistent than gold.

All 12 trades were winners, and all but three were in double digits. The compounded return during the approximately 19.33 years when investors actually held long-term Treasuries was 13.32 percent.

Yet gold fell on hard times from January 1990 to March 2000, a period which contained four separate buys and sells. Its stand-alone NAV, which began the period at 12,304, fell to 9895 in early 2000—a drawdown of (19.58) percent. However, if we look at Table 10-2, which includes the combined gold and long-term bond trades, investors never actually felt that loss.

Table 10-2 Gold and Long-Term Treasuries: Buy and Replace

	DATE	BUY	DATE	SELL	GAIN/(LOSS)%	NAV 1000
1.	12/31/71 G	43.625	11/14/73	90.00	+103.30	2063
2.	11/14/73 T	7.39	01/17/74	7.47	0.41	2071
3.	01/17/74 G	128.35	05/05/75	163.50	27.39	2638
4.	05/05/75 T	8.26	02/23/77	8.26	19.97	3165
5.	02/23/77 G	139.20	12/10/80	579.00	315.95	13,265
6.	12/10/80 T	12.85	09/07/82	12.29	32.58	17,454
7.	09/07/82 G	481.00	06/06/83	407.80	(15.22)	14,798
8.	06/06/83 T	11.06	01/14/86	9.75	45.19	21,484
9.	01/14/86 G	341.00	02/01/88	452.70	32.76	28,524
10.	02/01/88 T	8.34	01/12/90	8.14	17.16	33,418
11.	01/12/90 G	416.25	04/30/90	367.75	(11.65)	29,525
12.	04/30/90 T	9.02	05/13/93	6.49	58.98	46,939
13.	05/13/93 G	367.00	12/06/94	375.75	2.38	48,056
14.	12/06/94 T	7.93	01/05/96	6.11	29.76	62,358
15.	01/05/96 G	395.90	06/06/90	384.85	(2.79)	60,618
16.	06/06/96 T	7.08	09/28/99	6.47	30.12	78,876
17.	09/28/99 G	301.50	03/30/00	275.75	(8.54)	72,140
18.	03/30/00 T	6.26	09/17/01	5.44	19.00	85,947
19.	09/17/01 G	293.25	05/10/04	375.00	27.88	109,780

Table 10-2   Gold and Long-Term Treasuries: Buy and Replace *(Continued)*

	DATE	BUY	DATE	SELL	GAIN/(LOSS)%	NAV
20.	05/10/04 T	5.54	10/25/04	4.74	12.62	123,635
21.	10/25/04 G	429.15	10/10/06	573.30	33.59	165,164
22.	10/10/06 T	4.96	09/07/07	4.73	7.42	177,420
23.	09/07/07 G	701.00	08/08/08	852.50	21.61	215,760
24.	08/08/08 T	4.58	09/07/09	4.24	6.83	230,496
25.	09/07/09 G	993.00	12/31/10	1421.10	43.11	329,863
CMPD Return = 16.03						

G = Gold
T = Treasuries

The NAV for Treasuries, which was 2717 on January 12, 1990, had grown to 7293—that was the number on September 28, 1999, when investors exited the last Treasuries trade—by the time gold reached its low point on March 30, 2000, which was a gain of 168 percent for that period, easily erasing the gold loss and then some. And looking at Table 10-2, we can see that the cumulative NAV of gold and Treasuries together, which stood at 33,418 on January 12, 1990, before gold began its individual drawdown, reached 72,140 by the time gold's drawdown was over on March 30, 2000; this was an actual increase of 116 percent.

This B&R strategy also navigated the turbulent 2007–2009 period, which was made up of a gold trade followed by a Treasuries purchase, with relative ease. B&R picked up on the fact that the Fed, fearful subprime mortgage losses would prompt Wall Street to cut back on its flow of credit to businesses, was flooding the banking system with liquidity. B&R sent out the signal to switch out of long-term Treasuries and into gold on September 7, 2007. At the time gold was trading at 701.00, while the S&P 500 finished that day at 1453.55—see Table 10-1, section a—During the following 11 months gold performed admirably, while equities soon began to sink. When gold made a 6-month low on August 8, 2008, at 852.50, it still was 21.61 percent higher than its purchase price, and B&R investors switched into long-term Treasuries when their rate was 4.58. At the same time, the S&P 500 closed that day at 1296.32, which was off more than 10 percent from its starting point. And this was still before Lehman and the other garbage had hit the fan.

Soon after, the S&P 500 went into free fall, and by year-end, had shed another 30 percent. Meanwhile, B&R investors were safely ensconced in long-term government bonds, as falling rates propelled the bond price higher. By year-end, the long-term rate had fallen 1.53 basis points and B&R investors had an additional paper profit of 24.26 percent. At that time, B&H stock investors were sitting on a (37.5) percent paper loss since September 2007, while B&R investors were 51 percent winners.

But in early 2009, both long-term Treasuries and the S&P 500 reversed direction, allowing B&H stock investors to do some catching up. On September 7, 2009, which was Labor Day in the United States, gold gave its next signal to switch out of Treasuries, which was executed (for the 20-year Treasury) on the following day. Let's recap: The long-term bond, after giving back more than 70 percent of its 2008 gain, which worked out to a 14 percent intrayear drawdown, still delivered a 6.83 percent profit to August 2008 buyers. The final score for the whole 2-year period: B&H investors, even after including dividend income and a powerful 13.5 percent 2009 rally, down approximately 25 percent; B&R investors, up 29.91 percent.

Buy and Replace Annual Figures

Table 10-3 presents the results of the B&R strategy in annual figures.

Table 10-3   Gold and Long-Term Treasuries 1972–2010: Buy and Replace

YEAR	GOLD /B&R%	NAV 1000	G/T%	NAV 1000
1972	48.77	1488	27.2	1272
1973	40.11	2085	35.9	1729
1974	44.40	3011	35.2	2337
1975	(5.65)	2840	(7.8)	2155
1976	1675	3316	6.3	2291
1977	13.15	3752	10.9	2540
1978	37.00	5141	17.9	2995
1979	131.33	11,892	65.0	4942
1980	17.81	14,010	4.4	5159
1981	1.86	14,270	(15.4)	4365
1982	16.22	16,585	27.6	5569
1983	(12.70)	14,479	(7.9)	5129
1984	15.48	16,720	(1.8)	5037
1985	30.97	21,898	18.5	5969
1986	11.89	24,502	21.7	7264
1987	24.50	30,505	10.9	8056
1988	(5.51)	28,824	(2.8)	7830
1989	18.11	34,044	7.6	8425
1990	(0.94)	33,724	1.5	8552
1991	19.80	40,401	5.3	9005
1992	8.05	43,653	1.1	9104
1993	13.59	49,586	17.1	10,661
1994	(3.04)	48,078	(4.3)	10,202
1995	31.67	63,305	16.3	11,865
1996	3.64	65,609	(2.8)	11,533
1997	15.85	76,008	(2.8)	11,210
1998	13.06	85,935	6.1	11,894
1999	(11.08)	76,413	(4.0)	11,418
2000	6.69	81,525	7.9	12,320
2001	(0.31)	81,273	2.2	12,591

Table 10-3   Gold and Long-Term Treasuries (1972–2010): Buy and Replace *(Continued)*

YEAR	GOLD /B&R%	NAV 1000	G/T%	NAV 1000
2002	25.60	102,078	21.7	15,324
2003	19.90	122,392	10.6	16,948
2004	2.98	126,039	6.5	18,050
2005	17.70	148,348	12.7	20,342
2006	13.68	168,642	12.2	22,824
2007	26.01	212,506	21.1	27,640
2008	26.63	269,097	14.6	31,675
2009	(4.41)	257,230	6.3	33,670
2010	28.72	331,106	19.43	4064

	B&R	G/T	B&H
CMPD Return	16.04	9.96	10.05
T-Bill Return	5.56	5.56	5.56
Excess Return (ER)	10.48	4.40	4.49
Standard Deviation	23.87	14.78	18.33
Average Underperformance (2.55)	(3.39)	(5.10)	
Gain-to-Pain Ratio	4.11	1.30	0.88
Worst Drawdown	(12.70)	(15.37)	(37.61)
2nd Worst Drawdown	(11.08)	(7.83)	(37.25)
No. of Years Outperformed T-Bills	29	24	26

To review: This strategy delivered an impressive 39-year annualized return of 16.04 percent, which was more than half again higher than both B&H and G/T returns. B&R's total dollar return was approximately eight times as much as each of the two passive strategies. And it was able to do so while posting an impressively lower risk profile. Its average underperformance of (2.55) was about 25 percent below passive G/T's, and just one-half of B&H's (5.10) figure—quite a difference from a standard deviation that read 30 percent higher than an all-stocks portfolio. Moreover, its 4.11 G/P ratio left both G/T and B&H ratios of 1.30 and 0.88, respectively, in its dust. Worst drawdown comparisons were similar. B&R's worst stumble, on an annual basis, was (12.70) percent, while G/T's was (15.4) percent and B&H's (37.6) percent was almost three times as high. Also we should not overlook B&R's 74 percent of the time payoff for taking on risk, 29 of 39 years, beating B&H's 26 years.

This strategy also produced a larger return than B&S by more than a compounded 2 percent, 16.04[1] to 13.84 percent, which was enough to give investors a total dollar return that was twice as large. See Table 9–3.

However, its average underperformance (risk) of (2.55) was considerably above B&S's (1.71) percent. Consequently, its G/P lagged B&S's 4.82 number. Nonetheless, the 39-year results from this program were, in fact, stunning. Quite probably very few mutual funds, hedge funds, or individuals for that matter beat it. And on a risk-adjusted basis, that small number would shrink even further.

Oh, one more thing: Had we eliminated the supersized 1979 return of 131.33 percent as an aberration unlikely to repeat, we nevertheless would have received a 13.95 percent compounded return—still impressive. On the flip side of the coin, it would also have reduced gold B&R's standard deviation from 23.87 to a more modest 15.11, which then comes out about 18 percent below B&H's 18.33 percent number. Was B&R's stunning 1979 success really a penalty for success?

HOW GOOD WAS BUY AND REPLACE AS A SEARCH ENGINE?

Now we can ask the question: How well did our reverse 6-month/ 1-year algorithm work as a search engine in selecting the proper asset class, gold or long-term Treasuries? Table 10-4 includes the results from the selected trades alongside unselected returns.

Table 10-4   Gold and Long-Term Treasuries: Selected and Unselected Asset Comparison

	PERIOD	SELECTED ASSET	GAIN/ (LOSS) %	NAV 1000	UNSELECTED ASSET	GAIN/ (LOSS) (%)	NAV 1000
1.	12/31/71–11/14/73	G	**03.30**	2063	Tr	(3.37)	966
2.	11/14/73–01/17/74	Tr	+0.41	2071	G	**42.87**	1380
3.	01/17/74–05/05/75	G	**27.39**	2638	Tr	2.10	1409
4.	05/05/75–02/23/77	Tr	**19.97**	3165	G	(14.86)	1200
5.	02/23/77–12/10/80	G	**315.95**	13,265	Tr	(8.05)	1103
6.	12/10/80–09/07/82	Tr	**32.58**	17,454	G	(16.93)	916
7.	09/07/82–06/06/83	G	(15.22)	14,798	Tr	**18.70**	1088
8.	06/06/83–01/14/86	Tr	**45.19**	21,484	G	(16.38)	909
9.	01/14/86–02/01/88	G	32.76	28,524	Tr	**37.52**	1251
10.	02/01/88–01/12/90	Tr	**17.16**	33,418	G	(8.05)	1150
11.	01/12/90–04/30/90	G	(11.65)	29,525	Tr	**(5.66)**	1085
12.	04/30/90–05/13/93	Tr	**58.98**	46,939	G	(0.20)	1083
13.	05/13/93–12/06/94	G	**2.38**	48,056	Tr	(0.19)	1081
14.	12/06/94–01/05/96	Tr	**29.76**	62,358	G	5.36	1139
15.	01/05/96–06/06/96	G	**(2.79)**	60,618	Tr	(7.66)	1051
16.	06/06/96–09/28/99	Tr	**(30.12)**	78,876	G	(21.66)	824
17.	09/28/99–03/30/00	G	(8.54)	72,140	Tr	**5.70**	871
18.	03/30/00–09/17/01	Tr	**(19.00)**	85,947	G	6.35	926
19.	09/17/01–05/10/04	G	**27.88**	109,780	Tr	13.88	1048
20.	05/10/04–10/25/04	Tr	12.62	123,635	G	**14.44**	1199
21.	10/25/04–10/10/06	G	**33.59**	165,164	Tr	6.43	1276
22.	10/10/06–09/07/07	Tr	7.42	177,420	G	**22.27**	1561
23.	09/07/07–08/08/08	G	**21.61**	215,760	Tr	6.21	1658
24.	08/08/08–09/07/09	Tr	6.83	230,496	G	**16.48**	1931
25.	09/07/09–12/31/10*	G	**43.11**	329,863	Tr	6.79	2062

	SELECTED	UNSELECTED
CMPD Return	16.03	1.87
Outperformed	17	8
Times Profitable (Out of 25 Periods)	21	14
Total of All Losses	(38.20)	(103.01)

G = Gold
Tr = Treasuries
Outperformer during each year in **BOLD**

As we can see, our search engine selected the outperforming asset (in **bold**) 17 of its 25 tries. It missed eight times—one was a marginal miss of less than 3 percent—coming out to an error rate of about 32 percent, which for a financial search engine is quite low. The selected assets compounded total return was 16.03 percent. That stands in stark contrast to a measly compounded return of 1.87 percent for the unselected assets. Moreover, there were 12 times when the search engine had the choice to select either a positive or a negative return, and it made the right choice 10 of those times (or 83 percent). All in all, our 1-year/6-month algorithm certainly seems to have performed its job quite well.

To sum up: (1) gold or 20-year Treasuries has been a useful addition, supplementing equities, in an investment strategy and (2) B&R has worked quite well in directing investors to the better performer of the two.

The combination of gold and long-term Treasuries works so nicely because both assets usually respond to the same metric—actual or expected changes in the general price level—but in an opposing way, and as a result they display a high degree of negative correlation. The intriguing thing about this financial system B&R program is that, to my knowledge, it is generally ignored by the amateur and professional investment classes alike. Until they catch on, it could provide a nice investor edge.

In the next chapter, we take this 1-year/6-month search engine on to the REIT market and see if it can also improve upon a passive REIT return, as it did for the S&P 500, gold, and Treasuries.

CHAPTER 11

REAL ESTATE INVESTMENT TRUST TRENDS

I t has been said repeatedly, "the three most important things to look for in real estate are location, location, and location." But in looking back at the history of real estate, especially since World War II, what strikes us is appreciation, appreciation, and appreciation ... at least up until 2006.

The sixty years following World War II featured a robust bull market in real estate that would not quit. People and businesses, enriched by escalating incomes from an unusually long period of unparalleled prosperity, took some of their savings and used it for down payments on homes, condominiums, apartment buildings, factories, stores, and office buildings. With job and business opportunities multiplying, people and companies were on the move from cold-weather to sunshine state, from north to south, from city to suburb, from apartment to home, and from storefront to office building in the sky, providing ever more energy to fuel the property bull market. And, not to be overlooked, the government was riding shotgun for the rising real estate market, allowing generous tax breaks, legitimizing and abetting the use of *leverage* (20 percent down and even lower), and making sure that generous amounts of credit found its way to the property market. No wonder real estate was a good investment, and because of its leverage feature, it was often an *outstanding* investment ... again, until late 2006.

When real estate investment trusts (REITs) were introduced in the early 1960s, investors had a vehicle to capture some of those lush investment returns. The NAREIT All-Equity REIT Index dates back to 1972, but on a monthly basis only. They started putting out a daily index sometime in 1999, but as far as I know, they didn't maintain a record of the data. However, in early 2001, Cohen & Steers began publishing a daily index of 50 major REITs and formed ICF, an exchange-traded fund that tracked the index and has also done quite a good job of tracking the NAREIT Index.

Now we are going to see if our search engine also works on the last piece in the wealth chain, the property market. Prior to 2002, we will have to work off of monthly figures. While returns will be less precise than if we were able to use the daily numbers, they should still be in the ballpark. We will use the monthly NAREIT All-Equity REIT Index before 2002, and thereafter the daily Cohen & Steers 50 Majors Index, as reflected in the exchange-traded fund ICF.

ACTIVE REIT

Our next question is: Do we make the property market easier or harder to buy? Given its long-term record of continuous growth and the huge agent and institutional cheering section rooting for higher real estate prices, it seems to be a no-brainer to make REITs easier to buy and harder to sell. That means buying on a 6-month up and selling on a 1-year low and retreating into inter-mediate Treasuries, much we did with the S&P 500. Prior to 2002, we will use the 6-month/1-year algorithm on the monthly figures in the same manner as we did on the daily numbers. We will use adjusted prices as it includes dividend payments, which constitute a large portion of the total return. We will call this strategy ART (see Table 11-1).

Table 11-1   REITs: Buy and Sell*

	BUY	NAREIT INDEX	SELL	NAREIT INDEX	% PROFIT/ (LOSS)
1.	07/31/72	105.30	11/30/73	91.46	(13.14)
2.	01/31/75	81.82	10/31/87	754.91	822.65
3.	04/30/88	889.37	04/30/90	936.32	5.28
4.	02/28/91	947.73	10/31/94	1554.55	64.03
5.	05/31/95	1675.84	07/31/98	2681.98	60.04
6.	04/30/99	2586.46	10/31/99	2341.56	(9.47)
7.	03/31/00	2433.30	12/31/01	3421.00	
8.	12/31/01*	29.44	07/27/07	74.51	255.81†
9.	07/30/09	37.86	12/31/10	65.26	72.37

* Switch to ICF on 12/31/01. Prices are adjusted for splits and dividends.

†Cumulative: 03/31/00–12/31/01 = +40.69%; 12/31/01–07/27/07 = +153.09

As we can see, there were eight buys during the 39-year period. The ICF buy on December 31, 2001, was a switch from the monthly to the daily index and therefore a continuation of the March 31, 2000, purchase. Six of the eight purchases were profitable, and five, including the present one (which was still in process as of December 2010), returned in excess of 50 percent; two were well into triple digits. The largest loss was (13.14) following the July 1972 buy.

If we look at Table 11-2, we see that intermediate Treasuries outperformed REITs during five of the eight times investors were "out of the REIT market." Five-year yields fell—the note prices rallied—from the time of purchase to the time a new signal to shift back to REITs was given. During those 6¾ years, ART was "out of the REIT market," investors holding 5-year Treasuries reaped a compounded return of 8.00 percent for a total cumulative return of 68.2 percent. A 1682 NAV translates into 68.2 percent.

Table 11-2   Intermediate Treasury versus REIT Return: "Out of the Market" Performance

	BUY	YIELD	SELL	YIELD	NET YIELD/ CHANGE	INTERMEDIATE TREASURY RETURN	NAV 1000	REIT RETURN	NAV 1000
1.	12/31/71	5.50	07/31/72	5.98	+0.48	+1.33	1013	+11.05	1110
2.	11/30/73	6.80	01/31/75	7.34	0.54	4.55	1059	(10.54)*	993
3.	10/31/87	8.37	04/30/88	8.33	(0.04)	4.30	1105	17.81	1170
4.	04/30/90	9.04	02/28/91	7.66	(1.38)	12.31	1241	1.22	1185
5.	10/31/94	7.48	05/31/95	6.08	(1.40)	9.95	1364	7.80	1277
6.	07/31/98	5.52	04/30/99	5.24	(0.28)	4.85	1431	(3.56)	1232
7.	10/31/99	5.97	03/31/00	6.32	0.35	1.07	1446	3.92	1280
8.	07/27/07	4.60	07/30/09	2.66	(1.94)	16.30	1682	(48.02)	665

CMPD Return = 8.00% Intermediate Treasury return; 5.86% REIT return

Time invested in 5-year Treasuries = 6.75 years

Meanwhile, investors who hadn't paid attention to our algorithm's seven sell signals suffered through a compounded paper loss of (5.86) percent, which totaled (33.5) percent on a cumulative basis.

What was noteworthy was that investors had a buy alert for REITs at the end of March 2000 and were to remain in that asset category for more than 7 years. Most of that time, some pundits—and at times many of them—warned of a growing "bubble" in real estate. But ART followers were able to sit tight and ignore the debate about whether or not real estate prices were due for a precipitous fall. The sole metric they focused on, perhaps like a laser beam, was a 1-year low in the ICF exchange-traded fund. This low finally occurred on July 27, 2007, about 6 months after ICF's peak price, and it was still early in a bear market that was to turn into a debacle. Following the sell alert, prices cascaded another 69 percent. Nonetheless, ART investors would have pocketed a 255 percent return on their original March 2000 investment. Meanwhile, in March 2000, S&P 500 buyers would have been in the black by the whopping sum of 9 percent during that time period, and even that piddling amount depended on dividend income.

ACTIVE REITS' ANNUAL RESULTS

The annual results from ART, shown in Table 11-3, are every bit as striking as those from the other three asset classes: stocks, gold, and long-term Treasuries.

Table 11-3   Active REITs (ART) versus Passive REITs: Annual Returns

YEAR	ART RETURNS (%)	NAV 1000	PASSIVE REIT RETURNS (%)	NAV 1000
1972	(1.45)	985	8.01	1080
1973	(1.11)	975	(15.52)	913
1974	5.69	1030	(21.40)	717
1975	2.99	1061	19.30	856
1976	47.59	1566	47.59	1263
1977	22.42	1917	22.42	1546
1978	10.34	2115	10.34	1706
1979	35.86	2873	35.86	2317
1980	24.37	3573	24.37	2882
1981	6.00	3788	6.00	3055
1982	21.60	4606	21.60	3715
1983	30.64	6017	30.64	4853
1984	20.93	7277	20.93	5869
1985	19.10	8667	19.10	6989
1986	19.16	10,327	19.16	8328
1987	(7.98)	9503	(3.64)	8025
1988	5.19	9996	13.49	9107
1989	8.84	10,880	8.92	9920
1990	4.75	11,397	(15.41)	8391

Table 11-3   Active REITs (ARTs) versus Passive REITs: Annual Returns (Continued)

YEAR	ART RETURNS (%)	NAV	PASSIVE REIT RETURNS	NAV
1991	21.68	13,868	35.70	11,386
1992	14.59	15,891	14.59	13,047
1993	19.65	19,013	19.65	15,612
1994	(0.32)	18,953	3.17	16,107
1995	22.00	23,122	15.27	18,566
1996	35.27	31,277	25.27	25,113
1997	20.26	37,614	20.26	30,201
1998	(5.66)	35,485	(17.50)	24,916
1999	(11.55)	31,387	(4.62)	23,764
2000	25.52	39,397	26.37	30,030
2001	13.93	44,885	13.93	34,214
ICF begins*				
2002	2.98	46,222	3.82	35,521
2003	36.79	63,227	37.13	48,711
2004	35.22	85,496	31.58	64,093
2005	14.13	97,576	12.16	71,888
2006	39.03	135,660	35.06	97,093
2007	(10.97)	120,779	(15.69)	81,857
2008	13.11	136,613	(37.73)	50,974
2009	29.51	176,927	27.99	65,243
2010	28.16	226,750	27.95	83,478

	ART	PASSIVE REIT	S&P: B&H
CMPD Return	+14.92	12.01	+10.05
90-Day T-Bills	5.56	5.56	5.56
Excess Return	9.36	6.45	4.49
Standard Deviation	14.59	18.94	18.33
Aver. Underperformance	(2.34)	(4.74)	(5.10)
Gain-to-Pain Ratio	4.00	1.36	0.88
Worst Drawdown	(16.56)	(47.50)	(37.61)
2nd Worst Drawdown	(10.97)	(33.61)	(37.25)
No. of Yrs. Outperformed T-Bills	27	29	26

* Passive REIT numbers reflect NAREIT index, while ART's returns are based on ICF figures.

The compounded return of 14.92 percent was almost 3 percent better than a passive version of this asset-class strategy. It also handily beat the B&H's compounded return of 10.05 percent. The total dollar return on an initial $1000 investment was more than two and a half times better than its passive counterpart and more than five times greater than B&H. And in both cases, the ART did so with considerably less risk. Its average underperformance of (2.34) came in at one-half of the AU of the passive REIT and was just 46 percent of B&H's AU. The result was a G/P ratio of 4.00, way above both of the other passive strategies' G/P ratios, which were stuck at 1.36 (passive REIT) and 0.88 (B&H). The ART's worst drawdown of (16.56) also compared favorably to the passive REIT's (47.50) and the S&P 500's (37.61).

Obviously, ART was playing in the same league as both B&S and B&R. Its compounded return fell almost exactly midway between the annualized returns of the other two. Its AU was slightly below B&R, while above that of B&S. But most importantly, ART's stats, like those of B&S and B&R, lend credence to the fact that investors would have significantly increased performance by using our 6-month/1-year algorithm.

An intriguing question is how well did our active REIT investment do in the "bubble" bull market (from the beginning of 2000 to July 2007), as compared to the returns active real estate speculators were pocketing during that period? Certainly the 255 percent return beat the average nonleveraged real estate investment, which was around 83 percent according to the Case-Shiller National Real Estate Index during that time frame, and that's without requiring all the work active investors had to do. Also, ART participants were able to easily liquidate in July 2007 while active real estate investors had trouble selling many of their properties that had not already been unloaded. And some of the losses bag-holding real estate speculators took, or are sitting on, are humongous.

HIGHLY LEVERAGED SPECULATORS

On the other hand, many active real estate speculators took advantage of the generous amounts of credit available and leveraged way up, even more so than the traditional 5:1 (based on a 20 percent down payment) ratio. Furthermore, highly leveraged speculators—if they concentrated on the "hot" states of Nevada, Florida, Arizona, or (Southern) California and had either pocketed enough early profits or were able to dump their inventory not too long after real estate turned south—should have done quite well and easily beaten the 255 percent REIT return.

That said, there was no reason why ART followers also couldn't have leveraged up, although not to the degree of the active speculators, and increased those already generous returns, with no legwork or illiquidity problems to boot. In Chapter 14, we introduce a leveraged ART portfolio to compare with the hypothetical returns active real estate investors were likely receiving during the first decade of the twenty-first century.

In the next chapter, we put all three active strategies together into one combined portfolio.

CHAPTER 12

AN ACTIVE COMBINED ASSET STRATEGY

Now we can put the three active strategies together. We are going to split all three programs equally. (Other divisions, such as one-half in B&R, as it represents two asset classes, and one-fourth in each of the other two, wouldn't move the result needle very much.) I will call this portfolio the active combined asset (ACA) portfolio, and rebalance each year-end (see Table 12-1).

ACTIVE COMBINED ASSET PORTFOLIO

As the reader can easily see, ACA's 39-year compounded return of 15.58 percent was quite impressive. It beat its passive counterpart, PCA, which had a compounded return of 11.34 percent, as shown in Chapter 6, by more than 4 percent and blew away the buy-and-hold return of 10.05 percent by over 5.5 percent. Also, ACA's total return of $283,708 on an initial $1000 investment was more than four times higher than PCA's total dollar return and six and a half times greater than B&H's total dollar return. Moreover, it bested a riskless 90-day T-Bill investment in 33 of the 39 years; that is, ACA investors were paid to take on risk 85 percent of the time. If you remember, B&H players were paid for taking risk only 67 percent of the time (26 out of 39 years).

Table 12-1   Active Combined Asset (ACA) Portfolio: Annual Results

YEAR	B&S	B&R	ART	ACA	NAV 1000	T-BILL
1972	18.99	48.77	(1.45)	22.10	1221	3.84
1973	(5.44)	40.11	(1.11)	11.19	1358	6.93
1974	5.69	44.40	5.69	18.59	1610	8.00
1975	18.66	(5.65)	2.99	5.33	1696	5.80
1976	23.93	16.75	47.59	29.42	2195	5.08
1977	(4.47)	13.15	22.42	10.37	2422	5.12
1978	3.85	37.00	10.34	17.06	2836	7.18
1979	18.61	131.33	35.86	61.93	4592	10.38
1980	32.50	17.81	24.37	24.89	5735	11.24
1981	5.29	1.86	6.00	4.38	5987	14.71
1982	35.75	16.22	21.60	24.52	7455	10.54
1983	22.56	(12.70)	30.64	13.50	8461	8.90
1984	4.77	15.48	20.93	13.73	9623	9.85
1985	31.73	30.97	19.10	27.27	12,246	7.72
1986	18.67	11.89	19.16	16.57	14,276	6.16
1987	2.63	24.50	(7.98)	6.38	15,187	5.47
1988	7.34	(5.51)	5.19	2.34	15,543	6.35
1989	31.69	18.11	8.84	19.55	18,581	8.37
1990	(0.82)	(0.94)	4.75	1.00	18,766	7.81
1991	24.99	19.80	21.68	22.16	22,924	5.60
1992	7.62	8.05	14.59	10.09	25,236	3.51
1993	10.08	13.59	19.65	14.44	28,880	2.90
1994	1.32	(3.04)	(0.32)	(0.68)	28,684	3.90
1995	37.58	31.67	22.00	30.42	37,408	5.60
1996	22.96	3.64	35.27	20.62	45,123	5.21
1997	33.36	15.85	20.26	23.16	55,572	5.26
1998	28.58	13.06	(5.66)	11.99	62,237	4.86
1999	21.04	(11.08)	(11.55)	(0.53)	61,908	4.68
2000	(6.09)	6.69	25.52	8.71	67,298	5.89
2001	7.62	(0.31)	13.93	7.08	72,062	3.83

Table 12-1 Active Combined Asset (ACA) Portfolio: Annual Results *(Continued)*

YEAR	B&S	B&R	ART	ACA	NAV	T-BILL
ICF Begins						
2002	12.93	25.60	3.26	13.93	82,101	1.65
2003	21.12	19.90	37.57	26.20	103,608	1.02
2004	10.88	2.98	34.67	16.18	120,369	1.20
2005	4.91	17.70	14.54	12.38	135,274	2.98
2006	15.79	13.68	38.54	22.67	165,941	4.80
2007	5.49	26.01	(10.97)	6.84	177,297	4.66
2008	1.57	26.63	13.11	13.77	201,711	1.60
2009	15.24	(4.41)	29.51	13.45	228,834	0.10
2010	15.06	28.72	28.16	23.98	283,708	0.12

	90-DAY T-BILL	B&S	B&R	ART	ACA
CMPD Return	+5.56%	+13.84	+16.01	+14.85	+15.58
Excess Return	—	+8.28	+10.45	+9.29	+10.02
Risk Measures					
Standard Deviation		12.11	23.87	14.59	11.27
Avg. Underperformance		(1.71)	(2.55)	(2.34)	(0.81)
Gain-to-Pain Ratio		4.84	4.10	3.97	12.37
Worst Drawdown		(6.09)	(12.70)	(16.56)	(0.68)
2nd Drawdown		(5.44)	(11.08)	(10.97)	(0.53)
No. Yrs. Outperformed					
T-Bills		28	29	27	33

Risk Profile

Now let's take a look at ACA's risk profile. We'll begin with a "hard-to-believe" average underperformance of (0.81) percent, which was just 50 percent of the PCA's AU and not even 16 percent of passive S&P 500's AU of (5.10). Does that mean it was 84 percent less risky than the S&P 500? Or, based on its standard deviation of 11.27 compared to the S&P 500's 18.33 percent, only 39 percent less risky? You choose!

Naturally, ACA's G/P ratio was off the chart at 12.37, which compared to 3.54 for PCA and a rather lowly 0.88 for B&H. Moreover, its worst drawdown loss, on an annual basis, was just (0.68) percent. That compares to PCA's at (11.37) percent; B&H had three drawdowns of over (37.00) percent. More telling was the fact that ACA's average underperformance came in 43 percent *less than* intermediate Treasuries, which sits right next to the 90-day T-Bill at the very bottom of the "risk" chain. The ACA strategy seems to have succeeded, beyond any seasoned investor's expectations, in the important matter of managing risk, even more so than obtaining superior returns . . . and that is quite significant for investment success.

Annual Component Returns

We also have 39 years of return data from each of the three portfolio components, for a total of 117 annual component returns. Eighty-four (72 percent) beat the 90-day T-Bill return and 42 returned in excess of 20 percent.

On the flip side of the coin, only 19 yearly returns (about 16 percent) were actually in the red, and just 4 reached double digits; ART's loss of (16.56) percent during the 1998–1999 period was the worst.

ACTIVE COMBINED ASSET PORTFOLIO VERSUS THE S&P 500

In Table 12-2, we split the S&P 500's buy-and-hold performance into two categories: first, when it beat the 90-day T-Bill return, and, second, when it fell short of the riskless return.

During the 26 years when equity risk was being rewarded (stocks beat T-Bills), the S&P 500 performed admirably, beating the ACA in 15 of the 26 years, and posted a compounded return of 21.68 percent, handily outperforming T-Bills by a margin of 16.46 percent. Meanwhile, ACA, which also beat T-Bills, but by

Table 12-2   Active Combined Asset (ACA) versus S&P 500

A. WHEN S&P 500 BEAT RISKLESS 90-DAY T-BILLS

YEAR	ACA	NAV 1000	S&P	NAV 1000	T-BILL %	NAV 1000
1972	24.76	1248	18.99	1190	3.84	1038
1975	4.23	1300	37.23	1633	5.80	1098
1976	28.15	1666	23.93	2024	5.08	1154
1979	68.87	2813	18.61	2401	10.38	1274
1980	23.69	3480	32.50	3181	11.24	1417
1982	23.35	4292	21.55	3866	10.54	1566
1983	10.88	4759	22.56	4739	8.90	1706
1985	27.63	6074	31.73	6242	7.72	1837
1986	16.10	7052	18.67	7408	6.16	1951
1988	1.55	7162	16.61	8638	6.35	2074
1989	19.40	8551	31.69	11,375	8.37	2248
1991	21.92	10,426	30.47	14841	5.60	2374
1992	9.88	11,456	7.62	15,972	3.51	2457
1993	14.35	13,099	10.08	17,582	2.90	2529
1995	30.54	17,100	37.58	24,190	5.60	2670
1996	18.92	20,335	22.96	29,744	5.21	2810
1997	22.42	24,895	33.36	39,666	5.26	2958
1998	12.10	27,907	28.58	51,003	4.86	3101
1999	(1.59)	27,463	21.04	61,734	4.68	3246
2003	25.56	34,483	28.68	79,439	1.02	3280
2004	13.85	39,258	10.88	88,082	1.20	3319
2005	12.91	44,327	4.91	92,407	2.98	3419
2006	21.77	53,977	15.79	106,998	4.80	3582
2007	7.11	57,814	5.49	112,873	4.66	3749
2009	11.66	64,556	26.46	142,739	0.10	3753
2010	23.98	80,037	15.06	164,235	0.12	3758
CMPD Return	+18.36%		+21.68%		5.22%	
T-Bill Rate	+13.14		+16.46			

Table 12-2   Active Combined Asset (ACA) versus S&P 500 (Continued)

B. WHEN S&P 500 TRAILED RISKLESS 90-DAY T-BILLS

YEAR	ACA	NAV	S&P	NAV	T-BILL	NAV
1973	+14.07	1141	(14.69)	853	+6.93	1069
1974	21.17	1382	(26.47)	627	8.00	1155
1977	10.64	1529	(7.16)	582	5.12	1214
1978	19.05	1820	6.57	620	7.18	1301
1981	4.13	1895	(4.92)	590	14.71	1493
1984	13.90	2159	6.27	627	9.85	1640
1987	8.19	2336	5.25	660	5.47	1729
1990	0.80	2354	(3.10)	640	7.81	1864
1994	(0.92)	2333	1.32	648	3.90	1937
2000	8.50	2531	(9.10)	589	5.89	2051
2001	6.34	2692	(11.89)	519	3.83	2130
2002	15.09	3098	(22.10)	404	1.65	2165
2008	15.05	3564	(37.00)	255	1.60	2199
CMPD Return	10.27		(9.98)		6.25	
T-Bill Rate	4.02		(16.23)			

a more modest 13.14 percent, trailed the S&P 500 return by 3.32 percent. That lag resulted in a total 26-year return that was only 49 percent of the S&P 500. No doubt that would have left some ACA investors impatient, especially during the 5-year 1995–99 time span when the S&P 500 compounded at a 28.55 percent rate, outdistancing ACA's more tepid return of 15.96 percent. However, when it does not pay to take on traditional equity risk, the picture changes dramatically.

During the 13 years the S&P 500 lost out to riskless T-Bills, their relative performance flipped; ACA beat the S&P 500 in 12 of the 13 years, and during that whole period an all-stock portfolio shrank at a compounded rate of (9.98) percent, which was a bone-chilling 16.23 percent worse than a riskless investment. Had those 13 years been consecutive, an investor would have ended the period 74.5 percent poorer. Meanwhile ACA was clearly operating in a different universe. Its compounded return of 10.26 percent was a full 4 percent higher than that of three-month T-Bills. Moreover, investors would have emerged from this "make-believe" consecutive period 256.4 percent richer. And this was the essence of ACA's overall risk-and-return outperformance.

By the way, if we look at Table 12-3 we can see that more than 61 percent of the time, 24 of the 39 years, all three of the pieces were in the black. In another 11 years, 28 percent, two of the components were profitable. In the remaining 4 years, only one of the parts, 10 percent, had a positive return.

Table 12-3   Number of Positive Components/Number of Years

	NUMBER OF YEARS	PERCENTAGE
All 3 in the black	24	61.5
2 in the black	11	28.0
1 positive component	4	10.0
No positive components	0	0.0

Active Combined Asset Portfolio During 2008

The year 2008 provides a good example to see how the active combined asset (ACA) portfolio works when the stock market is having a hard time. ACA investors began that year with a portfolio that was a third gold, a third S&P 500, and the remaining third in intermediate Treasuries. (The REIT trend had turned down in the summer of 2007.) The first shift came on January 16, when the S&P 500 made a 1-year low, which called for ACA investors to exit stocks and shift the money into 5-year Treasuries. At that point, gold was up nearly 6.4 percent and 5-year Treasuries were also ahead by about 2.5 percent; together this more than offset the 6.5 percent S&P 500 loss. All told, investors were up approximately 0.80 percent at that point.

Then on August 8, with the S&P 500 off about 11 percent for the year to date, we got the signal to sell gold and shift B&R's cash into long-term Treasuries. Since mid-January gold had given up a bit more than 4 percent, while 5-year Treasuries had returned about 85 basis points, leaving ACA's year-to-date return hovering at about even.

ACA investors, then fully committed to U.S. Treasuries (about 60.5 percent intermediate and 39.5 percent long-term Treasuries), were able to escape the carnage that would later devastate other risk-taking investors. During the remainder of the year, Lehman went bust, credit markets froze, financial markets seized up, and the S&P 500 tumbled another 30 percent. Meanwhile, the Fed was frantically pushing interest rates lower; Treasuries across the broad soared, producing a blended (intermediate and long-term) return of more than 13.5 percent. This put the ACA portfolio solidly in the money for 2008, with a return of 13.77 percent.

THE REASON FOR THE ACA PORTFOLIO'S SUPERIOR PERFORMANCE

The ACA portfolio's excellent performance owes much to the fact it is founded on the basic building blocks of our wealth-generating system and the "variation" it provides. But it owes even more to the fact that in games of uncertainty people herd—and that herding results in up-and-down trends, which are fed by a phalanx of corresponding feedback loops. Knowledge of the direction of the feedback loops, provided by our 1-year, 6-month algorithm, usually enables investors to see multiple loops into the future, typically surpassing predictions based on analyzing the internal fundamentals of the market. While the former counts on a simple key variable, the direction of the trend, to define the component relationships, the latter attempts the improbable task of making sense of all of the shifting relationships between numerous interacting components.

As in most cases wherein human knowledge is limited, simplicity beats out complexity. And we have 39 years of investment market history, wherein our 6-month/1-year algorithm has worked as a rule of market rhythm, to prove the point. And it enabled followers to co-opt and take advantage of system fluctuation, rather than being its victim.

In the next chapter, we will go on to our own unique problem, a risk profile that may be too low.

CHAPTER 13

RISK: TAKING
ON MORE?

Most investment books eventually come to a place wherein they introduce the concept of "risk" and how to control or manage it. Stock/Bond 60/40, first discussed in Chapter 2 is such an attempt. To refresh memories, we showed how the 60 percent stock/40 percent bond setup reduced the B&H portfolio's average underperformance to (2.80) and had only two drawdowns that went beyond 20 percent into "torture" territory, one being a skimpy (0.39) percent beyond. *But the ACA portfolio is already there, since controlling risk was built into its DNA.* Our problem is exactly the opposite: Shall we increase risk?

Over the past 39 years, an investment in intermediate government bonds had an average underperformance to "riskless" 3-month T-Bills of (1.42), which is about as far down the "risk" chain as you can go, except for very short-term Treasuries and ACA, which sported a puny AU of just (0.81) percent.

Many investors would be quite pleased with ACA's risk/reward attributes and willing to drop the matter of controlling risk before they got this far. More aggressive investors, however, might view ACA's low risk profile as an opportunity to stretch the return. Keep in mind increasing one's risk assumption to a more traditional level is a *significantly different* matter from taking on more than the normal amount of risk in search of mouthwatering returns.

ADDING LEVERAGE

The most common way to increase risk is by adding *leverage*, in which you borrow additional money to bump up your investment funds. There is, of course, a cost investors must pay to borrow the extra cash. That charge is usually tied to the Federal Funds Rate. We can get an approximate cost for borrowing funds by looking at the rates Interactive Brokers, a financial company that is an aggressive solicitor of leverage-using speculators, charge. As of this writing, they are willing to lend at a rate of from 0.25 to 1.50 percent above the Federal Funds Rate. Investors with less than $100,000 are charged 1.50 percent; from $100,000 to $1,000,000 the rate is 1.00 percent; from $1,000,000 to $3,000,000 the rate is 0.50 percent; and above $3,000,000 the cost of borrowing is only 0.25 percent.

The 90-day T-Bill rate has averaged a bit less than 20 basis points below the Federal Funds Rate during the past 20 years. So if we add the 20 basis point difference between the two to the 1.5 percent margin fee smaller investors would pay, we get an annual cost to borrow of approximately 1.7 percent over the rate on 90-day T-Bills. Naturally, investors with more than $100,000 would pay less and their returns would reflect the lower cost of borrowing. Their average underperformance would also come in lower.

The next decision is how much money to borrow. Leveraging an investment is a subtle matter; done intelligently, it can boost returns significantly, but if not executed carefully, it can be a one-way ticket to the poorhouse. A portfolio levered at a 2:1 ratio means you are doubling your original investment via borrowed funds; a 1.5:1 ratio indicates you have borrowed an amount of funds equal to only one-half of your original starting capital, and so on.

Selecting the Proper Amount

There are several considerations in selecting the proper amount of leverage. First, determine the average cost of borrowing.

That's easy! During the past 39 years, the T-bill return has been 5.56 percent. Add 1.70 percent to that figure and it comes out to about 7.26 percent.

Next, the compounded rate of return on the strategy you are considering levering should be well over the 7.26 percent cost of borrowing, say, at least one-third more.

The third, and most important, consideration is to determine what is an appropriate safe level of risk and how to get there. I would use the AU figure to calibrate the leverage level. In order to maintain a risk profile that is still considerably below that of the S&P 500, I would set an upper limit as to how high I would allow a levered AU to reach. One-half of the cost of borrowed money— 3.63, or 7.26/2—seems tolerable, i.e., not too risky.

Tables 13-1a and 13-1b show the headline results of leveraging our four most important programs; first at 2:1 (Table 13-1a) and then again at 1.5:1 (Table 13-1b).

As we can see, a lever of 2:1 increases average underperformances by an average of 126 percent; this means unleveraged AUs of about (1.60) or lower are likely to remain under the 3.63 ceiling: 1.60 × 2.26, adding 1% to 1.26%, resulting in 3.616. The average increase in AU for a 1.5:1 leverage ratio is 62 percent; this indicates unlevered AUs of approximately 2.24 and less will usually stay below the 3.63 threshold. Therefore, an intelligent user of leverage would probably not lever under these circumstances:

- With AUs of more than marginally above (1.60), at 2:1
- With AUs a bit higher than (2.24), at 1.5:1

One note: Obviously we are using AU and compounded return numbers derived in 2011, for use in earlier years, or before these figures were actually known. However, I do not think the earlier actual numbers (except for the very early years when investors would have had to rely on estimates) would have changed the results materially.

Table 13-1a   Adding Leverage at Levered 2:1

	S&P 500	ACA	PCA	AIP
Unlevered AU	(5.10)	(0.81)	(1.62)	(1.99)
Levered 2:1	**(10.82)**	**(1.87)**	**(3.76)**	**(4.59)**
Percent Increase AU	112	130	132	131
CMPD Return	8.20	23.06	14.46	14.27
Return Increase	(22.38)	45.16	27.51	26.28
Worst Drawdown	(84.20)	(7.64)	(31.41)	(32.88)

Avg. AU increase = +126%
Note: An average underperformance of 1.60 or less translates into a leveraged AU of less than 3.63%.

Table 13-1b   Adding Leverage at Levered 1.5:1*

	S&P	ACA	PCA	AIP
Unlevered AU	(5.10)	(0.81)	(1.62)	(1.99
Levered 1.5:1	**(7.94)**	**(1.33)**	**(2.65)**	**(3.27)**
Percent Increase AU	56	64	64	64
CMPD Return	**8.09**	**19.42**	**12.98**	**12.93**
Return Increase	(2.72)	23.84	13.14	13.59
Worst Drawdown	(60.42)	(5.62)	(19.51)	(20.55)

Avg. AU increase = +62%
*An AU of 2.24 or less translates into a levered AU of 3.63% or less.

Rebalancing versus Drift?

The final decision is whether to rebalance on an annual basis or allow for leverage drift. Anytime the investor does not rebalance at the end of the year, the leverage ratio drifts (deviates) up or down. Suppose you have a $2000 portfolio, 50 percent personal equity and 50 percent borrowed funds. A 2:1 lever makes $250, or 12.5 percent, during a calendar year. The investor would then have $1250 in personal equity, while borrowings would still total $1000. If the investor doesn't rebalance, by borrowing an additional $250 to match her winnings, she becomes subject to leverage drift. The portfolio would, in actuality, now be leveraged at a 1.8:1 ratio. Investor equity of $1250 plus $1000 of borrowed funds = $2250, divided by $1250 = 1.8.

After a losing year, leverage drift goes the other way. A 10 percent drawdown would amount to an actual 20 percent loss of the investor's stake. An investor who began the year with $2000 would be left with only $800 in personal equity, while borrowings would remain at $1000, a 2.25:1 ratio. To prevent leverage drift, the investor would have to sell off $200 of equities to bring borrowings down to $800.

Upside leverage drift based on diminishing investor equity would eventually, if not corrected for, set off Federal Reserve Board Regulation T, which requires investors to maintain equity levels at 25 percent or more of the total investment. If equity falls below that level, the investor is required to either add enough funds or sell off investments to bring the level back to the 25 percent marker.

ACA had a compounded return of more than two times the average cost of borrowing and an AU of a meager (0.81) percent. Yet I'm going to be quite conservative and margin it at a 2:1 ratio and rebalance at each year-end, back to that same leverage ratio. I will call this leveraged active combined assets L:ACA.

LEVERAGED ACTIVE COMBINED ASSET

At a 2:1 lever, the 39-year compounded return increases to 23.06 percent, which is 48 percent above the ACA number and more than double the B&H compounded return. See Table 13-2.

The portfolio's enormous $3,271,370 payoff at period's end on an initial $1000 investment was more than eleven and a half times that of ACA and greater than 78 times the S&P

Table 13-2   A 2:1 Leveraged ACA Portfolio (L:ACA)

YEAR	ACA 2:1 (%)	LESS T-BILL +1.7 (%)	TOTAL (%)	NAV 1000
1972	44.21%	(5.54)	38.67	1387
1973	22.37	(8.63)	13.74	1577
1974	37.19	(9.70)	27.49	2011
1975	10.67	(7.50)	3.17	2074
1976	58.85	(6.78)	52.07	3155
1977	20.73	(6.82)	13.91	3593
1978	34.13	(8.88)	25.25	4501
1979	123.87	(12.08)	111.79	9532
1980	49.79	(12.94)	36.85	13,044
1981	8.77	(16.41)	(7.64)	12,047
1982	49.05	(12.28)	36.77	16,476
1983	27.00	(10.60)	16.40	19,178
1984	27.45	(11.55)	15.90	22,228
1985	54.53	(9.42)	45.11	32,256
1986	33.15	(7.86)	25.29	40,413
1987	12.77	(7.17)	5.60	42,675
1988	4.68	(8.05)	(3.37)	41,236
1989	39.09	(10.07)	29.02	53,205
1990	1.99	(9.51)	(7.52)	49,205
1991	44.31	(7.30)	37.01	67,418
1992	20.17	(5.21)	14.96	77,506
1993	28.88	(4.60)	24.28	96,324
1994	(1.36)	(5.60)	(6.96)	89,620
1995	60.83	(7.30)	53.53	137,597
1996	41.25	(6.91)	34.34	184,843
1997	46.31	(6.96)	39.35	257,585
1998	23.99	(6.56)	17.43	302,474
1999	(1.06)	(6.48)	(7.54)	279,667
2000	17.41	(7.59)	9.82	307,140

Table 13-2   A 2:1 Leveraged ACA Portfolio (L:ACA) (Continued)

YEAR	ACA 2:1 (%)	LESS T-BILL +1.7 (%)	TOTAL (%)	NAV
2001	14.16	(5.53)	8.63	333,646
2002	27.86	(3.35)	24.51	415,423
2003	52.39	(2.72)	49.67	621,777
2004	32.35	(2.90)	29.45	804,911
2005	24.77	(4.68)	20.09	966,591
2006	45.34	(6.50)	38.84	1,342,015
2007	13.69	(6.36)	7.33	1,440,340
2008	27.54	(3.30)	24.24	1,789,478
2009	26.89	(1.80)	25.09	2,238,518
2010	47.96	(1.82)	46.14	3,271,370

	L:ACA	ACA
CMPD Return (%)	23.06	15.58
Excess Return	17.50	10.02
Average Underperformance	(1.87)	(0.81)
Standard Deviation	22.32	11.27
Gain-to-Pain Ratio	9.36	12.37
Worst Drawdown	(7.64)	(0.68)

500 result. Moreover, its AU clocked in at (1.87), only about 37 percent of the S&P 500 buy-and-hold figure and still about 48 percent shy of the (3.63) ceiling. However, its standard deviation at 22.32 was about 22 percent higher than S&P 500's. L:ACA's worst drawdown on an annual basis was only (7.64). For comparison purposes, the S&P 500 exceeded that level three times during the last 39 years. Also, L: ACA investors suffered through only 5 losing years as compared to 9 years for the S&P 500. Finally, ACA returns improved in 29 years, while only 3 winning years turned into losers.

During its 39-year period of existence, L:ACA's 23.06 percent compounded rate of return beat the 21.14 percent figure (during the comparable period) of legendary Warren Buffett's investment vehicle, Berkshire Hathaway. Levered ACA's total return of $3,271,370 was more than 84 percent greater than that of Berkshire Hathaway. Also, the average underperformance of L:ACA, (1.87) percent, was less than half of the approximate (4.50) percent AU of Berkshire Hathaway. Furthermore, Berkshire Hathaway suffered two drawdowns in excess of 20 percent, which exposed its investors to a combined (37.4) percent of torture. Incidentally, the gain-to-pain ratio for Buffett's Berkshire Hathaway came out to a quite respectable 3.40, but it was only about 36 percent of L:ACA's G/P ratio of 9.36.

There is no doubt that L:ACA's use of leverage enhanced investment results considerably. But leverage can be a two-edged sword; use it indiscriminately and it may well sink your ship. To get an idea of an unwise use of leverage, let's be gutsy and try to lever the S&P 500 at a 2:1 ratio, even though we know its AU of (5.10) percent was already well above our upper limit of (3.63). However, its annualized return of 10.05 percent, more than one-third higher than the cost of borrowed funds, might be suggestive of some upside mileage.

The S&P 500 Leveraged at a 2:1 Ratio

The picture that emerges, as shown in Table 13-3, is an average underperformance of (10.82) percent, more than double the amount of unleveraged B&H, and well over the cost of borrowed funds. Additionally, investors had to sweat out three grueling drawdowns in excess of 70 percent; by the way the last one, which began in 2000, may not yet be over. However, that much higher risk profile was hardly surprising.

Yet, after putting up with the additional risk, you would expect it to enhance returns at least a bit. However, the compounded return actually slipped from 10.05 percent to 8.21 percent, and the

Table 13-3   S&P 500 Buy and Hold, Levered at 2:1

YEAR	S&P 500 2:1(%)	T-BILL + 1.7 (%)	TOTAL %	NAV 1000	POTHOLE DRAWDOWNS
1972	+37.98	(5.54)	32.44	1324	
1973	(29.78)	(8.63)	(38.41)	816	
1974	(52.94)	(9.70)	(62.64)	305	**(76.96)**
1975	74.46	(7.50)	66.96	509	
1976	47.86	(6.78)	41.08	718	
1977	(14.32)	(6.82)	(21.14)	566	
1978	13.14	(8.88)	4.26	590	
1979	37.22	(12.08)	25.14	739	
1980	65.00	(12.94)	52.06	1123	
1981	(9.84)	(16.41)	(26.25)	828	**(26.25)**
1982	43.10	(12.28)	30.86	1004	
1983	45.12	(10.60)	34.52	1458	
1984	12.54	(11.55)	0.99	1472	
1985	63.46	(9.42)	54.04	2267	
1986	37.34	(7.86)	29.48	2936	
1987	10.50	(7.17)	3.33	3034	
1988	33.22	(8.05)	25.17	3797	
1989	63.38	(10.07)	53.31	5821	
1990	(6.20)	(9.51)	(15.71)	4907	
1991	60.94	(7.30)	53.64	7539	
1992	15.24	(5.21)	10.03	8295	
1993	20.16	(4.60)	15.56	9586	
1994	2.64	(5.60)	(2.96)	9302	
1995	75.16	(7.30)	67.86	15,614	
1996	45.92	(6.91)	39.01	21,705	
1997	66.72	(6.96)	59.76	34,676	
1998	57.16	(6.56)	50.60	52,222	
1999	42.08	(6.48)	35.60	70,813	
2000	(18.20)	(7.59)	(25.79)	52,550	

Table 13-3   S&P 500 Buy and Hold, Levered at 2:1 *(Continued)*

YEAR	S&P 500 2:1(%)	T-BILL + 1.7 (%)	TOTAL	NAV	POTHOLE DRAWDOWNS
2001	(23.78)	(5.53)	(29.31)	37,148	
2002	(44.20)	(3.35)	(47.55)	19,484	**(72.49)**
2003	57.36	(2.72)	54.64	30,130	
2004	21.76	(2.90)	18.86	35,813	
2005	9.82	(4.68)	5.14	37,654	
2006	31.58	(6.50)	25.08	47,097	
2007	10.98	(6.36)	4.62	49,273	
2008	(74.00)	(3.30)	(77.30)	11,185	**(84.20)**
2009	52.92	(1.80)	51.12	16,903	
2010	30.12	(1.82)	28.30	21,687	

S&P 500 B&H	
CMPD Return	8.21
Excess Return	2.65
Aver. Underperformance	(10.82)
Gain-to-Pain Ratio	(0.24)
Worst Drawdown	(84.20)

total return for the whole period was nearly 50 percent lower—from 41,824 to 21,687; this was a good example of using leverage *unwisely*. Investors suffered a great deal of increased pain for a pay-off of less gain.

Why Levering the Active Combined Assets Portfolio Works

The reason levering the active combined assets portfolio at 2:1 worked so well was that its AU was an extremely low (0.81), which was just 11 percent of the 7.26 percent cost of borrowing (its annualized return was 15.58 percent and that helped too, but it wasn't the most important metric). On the other hand, the AU of the S&P 500 at (5.10) was about 70 percent of the cost of borrowing. No matter that its compounded return was also above the cost of borrowing, its AU hurdle was too high to overcome.

Now if we make ACA into a $3,000,000 or more hedge fund, levered at 3:1, with access to borrowed funds from Interactive Brokers at 0.25 percent over the Fed Funds Rate, the compounded return shoots up to 32.41 percent, while its AU remains fairly benign at (2.43) percent, still below the SB 60/40 portfolio's comparable 39-year number of (2.94). The worst drawdown on an annual basis becomes (17.17), still below the 20 percent "torture" threshold. And, if you can believe it, 39 years later, an original $1000 investment would have become *$56,900,727*. This hypothetical result blew away the B&H portfolio: it was 1,360 times greater and was even 200 times the ACA strategy.

Table 13-4   1.5:1 Levered PCA = L:PCA

YEAR	1.5 × PCA (%)	LESS 1/2 T-BILL + 1.7 (%)	TOTAL (%)	NAV 1000
1972	**30.4**	(2.77)	27.63	1276
1973	15.6	(4.32)	11.28	1420
1974	8.4	(4.85)	3.55	1471
1975	15.3	(3.75)	11.55	1641
1976	**31.5**	(3.39)	28.21	2103
1977	14.9	(3.41)	11.49	2345
1978	19.8	(4.44)	15.36	2705
1979	**79.1**	(6.04)	73.06	4682
1980	24.6	(6.47)	18.13	5530
1981	(11.3)	(8.21)	(19.51)	4451
1982	**36.9**	(6.24)	30.66	5816
1983	14.1	(5.30)	8.80	6328
1984	8.8	(5.78)	3.02	6530
1985	**32.8**	(4.71)	28.09	8365
1986	**30.4**	(3.93)	26.47	10,579

Table 13-4   1.5:1 Levered PCA = L:PCA *(Continued)*

YEAR	1.5 × PCA (%)	LESS 1/2 T-BILL +1.7	TOTAL (%)	NAV
1987	8.8	(3.59)	5.21	11,130
1988	9.3	(4.03)	5.27	11,716
1989	20.8	(5.04)	15.76	13,563
1990	(5.9)	(4.76)	(10.66)	12,117
1991	28.8	(3.65)	25.15	15,165
1993	24.0	(2.30)	21.70	18,456
1994	(1.7)	(2.80)	(4.50)	17,626
1995	**32.1**	(3.65)	28.45	22,640
1996	19.8	(3.46)	16.34	26,399
1997	18.0	(3.48)	14.52	30,163
1998	8.7	(3.28)	5.42	31,798
1999	3.1	(3.24)	(0.14)	31,754
2000	12.4	(3.80)	8.60	34,585
2001	2.4	(2.77)	(0.37)	34,357
2002	9.3	(1.68)	7.62	36,975
2003	**32.7**	(1.36)	31.34	48,563
2004	20.8	(1.45)	19.35	57,960
2005	15.9	(2.34)	13.56	65,819
2006	28.2	(3.25)	24.95	82,241
2007	12.0	(3.18)	8.82	89,495
2008	(17.3)	(1.65)	(18.95)	72,535
2009	25.0	(0.90)	24.10	90,016
2010	30.6	(0.91)	29.69	116,742

	L:PCA
CMPD Return	12.98
T-Bill Return	5.56
Excess Return	7.42
Aver. Underperformance	(2.65)
Gain-to-Pain Ratio	2.80
Worst Drawdown	(19.51)

Table 13-5   1.5:1 Levered AIP = L:AIP

YEAR	1.5 × AIP	LESS 1/2 T-BILL + 1.7	TOTAL	NAV 1000
1972	31.20	(2.77)	28.43	1284
1973	28.15	(4.32)	23.83	1590
1974	24.50	(4.85)	19.65	1903
1975	1.85	(3.75)	(1.90)	1867
1976	30.10	(3.39)	26.71	2365
1977	22.15	(3.41)	18.74	2808
1978	23.05	(4.44)	18.61	3331
1979	82.99	(6.04)	76.95	5894
1980	16.60	(6.47)	10.13	6491
1981	(12.35)	(8.21)	(20.55)	5157
1982	38.45	(6.14)	32.31	6823
1983	7.45	(5.30)	2.15	6970
1984	8.65	(5.78)	2.87	7170
1985	28.05	(4.71)	23.34	8843
1986	31.30	(3.93)	27.37	11,263
1987	9.10	(3.59)	5.51	11,884
1988	4.00	(4.03)	(0.03)	11,881
1989	12.00	(5.04)	6.96	12,709
1990	(6.15)	(4.76)	(10.90)	11,323
1991	23.20	(3.65)	19.55	13,536
1992	8.40	(2.61)	5.79	14,321
1993	26.95	(2.30)	24.65	17,850
1994	(2.70)	(2.80)	(5.50)	16,868
1995	24.00	(3.65)	20.35	20,301
1996	15.80	(3.46)	12.34	22,807
1997	7.35	(3.48)	3.87	23,689
1998	(2.60)	(3.28)	(5.88)	22,296
1999	(6.25)	(3.24)	(9.49)	20,180
2000	21.10	(3.80)	17.30	23,672
2001	9.15	(2.77)	6.38	25,183

Table 13-5   1.5:1 Levered AIP = L:AIP (Continued)

YEAR	1.5 × AIP	LESS 1/2 T-BILL + 1.7	TOTAL	NAV 1000
2002	23.60	(1.68)	21.92	30,704
2003	29.20	(1.36)	27.84	39,252
2004	22.35	(1.45)	20.90	47,454
2005	18.80	(2.34)	16.46	55,264
2006	29.75	(3.25)	26.50	69,908
2007	13.30	(3.18)	10.12	76,981
2008	(4.25)	(1.65)	(5.90)	72,440
2009	20.36	(0.90)	19.46	86,533
2010	33.40	(0.91)	32.49	114,648

	L:AIP (%)
CMPD Return	12.93
Excess Return	7.37
Average Underperformance	(3.27)
Gain-to-Pain Ratio	2.25
Worst Drawdown	(20.55)

In Tables 13-4 and 13-5, I levered PCA and AIP, which both had AUs that fell in the slot between (1.60) and (2.24) at the 1.5:1 ratio. PCA's compounded return increased from 11.34 percent to 12.98 percent, while its AU also increased from (1.62) to (2.65) percent. AIP's compounded return increased from 11.30 to 12.93 percent and its AU went from (1.99) to (3.27) percent. In both cases, AUs stayed well below the (3.63) marker. Taken together they tacked on an average of 64 percent to their AUs in return for an increase in compounded return averaging 14 percent.

Also, I would like to mention there are several exchange-traded funds that are calibrated to provide two times the asset classes return, and two times the loss, such as SSO (2X-SPY), URE (2X-VNQ), DGP (2X-GLD), and UBT (2X-TLT). However, their tracking history is rather limited, less than

5 years, as of 03/2011. Yet so far, from June 2009 to December 2010, they performed pretty much as expected, delivering returns of 172 percent to as much as 210 percent of their tracked index. A combined portfolio of SSO, URE, and DGP would have returned 45.69 percent during 2010, just a tad, or 1 percent, below L:ACA's 46.14 number.

To repeat: If you have a strategy with a relatively benign average underperformance and a good-sized excess return, upping the ante through the use of leverage can boost returns materially. On the other hand, be aware that using leverage indiscriminately can lead to the destruction of your nest egg, and quite quickly.

THE RISK OF RUIN: DEVELOPING A CRISIS PLAN

Before finishing this chapter on risk, I want to return to another type of "risk," which I called the "risk of ruin." Earlier, I labeled the main strategy investors typically used (unconsciously) in dealing with a large unexpected paper loss as "panicking." Now I want to talk about having a crisis plan in place so as to avoid letting a falling market scare you into dumping your risk assets after a big market break.

The starting point for any such plan is to have a preset wealth-loss barrier, and preferably a second one also at a further distance. When the first barrier is breached, say at 20 percent (any other well-thought-out number will do), the investor would become more defensive, shifting money from offensive, risk-taking investments to defensive, safe assets. And a break of the second threshold, say at about the 50 percent mark, should spur investors to become even more defensive.

My own preference for ultrasafe defensive holdings would include:

- Treasury bills (T-Bills)
- TIPS (Treasury Inflation-Protected Securities)

- Intermediate (5-year) government notes
- CDs (5-year or less) at large well-capitalized banks
- Fixed (not variable, as we are talking about the reliability of the rate of return) annuities underwritten by a strong institution, if you are over age 60

The idea is to choose assets as rock solid as possible to weather the very worst of storms.

It's also a good idea to keep track of the offensive/defensive character of your investments and tailor the ratio between the two to your age (and your spouse's age, if applicable). To state the obvious, older investors should have higher defensive to offensive ratios than younger investors. In addition, as we all know, the ratio should also be based on a *realistic* assessment of your risk tolerance and respective earnings prospects for the remainder of your life. And it would be a good plan to rebalance back to that ratio at each year-end.

Then when facing a crisis situation, such as in 2008 when many investors were caught flat-footed and sold out near the bottom, a better strategy would be to reassess your offensive/defensive ratio and decide on how much to raise the defensive portion. This reassessment process can be thought of as a "modified" panic.

For example, suppose you are married, and you and your spouse are both 50 years old. You have an offensive/defensive ratio of 60/40, which means $600,000 of your $1 million investment portfolio is designated to risk-taking assets and the other $400,000 is deployed in safe, defensive investments. In addition, you don't want to see your net investment worth slip by more than 20 percent. Then along comes 2008 and at the end of November, when reviewing your monthly statements, you see your net investment worth has fallen 25 percent; according to plan that calls for you to take action.

Your calculations show the offensive portion of your investments is down 35 percent, to $390,000, while the defensive portion is off only 10 percent, to $360,000. Given the prevailing level of uncertainty accompanied by the noxious smell of fear throughout the land, you and your spouse decide to flip your ratio to 40/60. That requires a shift of $90,000 from offensive to defensive investments, which puts you at $300,000 offensive and $450,000 defensive. At that same time, you jointly decide that if your family net worth slips past the 50 percent barrier, you will retreat to a 20/80, offensive to defensive stance.

From the vantage point of year-end 2010, with the S&P 500 up about 40 percent from your switch date, that shift did not seem to help you. But that tilt into a more defensive mode might have allowed you to keep your head in late February 2009—when the stock market was down still another 17 percent and you saw extreme panic all around you—and perhaps actually shift a small portion of your assets (maybe on the order of $30,000) back to the offensive piece of your portfolio. This shift would maintain your 40/60 allocation (because the defensive portion of your portfolio probably fell less than the risk segment). By the time December 2010 rolled around, that particular move looked good. But most importantly, switching from 60 percent offense to only 40 percent in late 2008, and knowing that the bulk of your family wealth was now as safe as could be, may well have provided the confidence necessary to prevent you from joining in a wholesale "sell all risk assets" panic.

Investors can, of course, choose other methods, or other ratios, to protect themselves from an unexpected blow to their net worth, but the main point is they should have some preset plan in place. The above is just a suggestion to start investors thinking about preparing such a plan.

In the next chapter, we take this knowledge of leverage and turn our attention to real estate, in particular its spectacular "bubble" at the very beginning of the twenty-first century and the part leverage played in it.

CHAPTER 14

The Twenty-First Century "Real Estate" Bubble

Now that we have some idea of how leverage can be used intelligently or recklessly, let us return to that "Golden Age" of leveraging homes and condos from the turn of the twenty-first century until late 2006. It was the "Wild West" period in the property market, with gunslinging speculators roaming the real estate range in hopes of striking it rich. And many did ... at least for a while.

To get an idea of how profitable residential real estate was during that go-go period, we can consult the Case-Shiller National Home Price Index (CSI). The index was developed by economists Karl Case and Robert Shiller to study price trends by comparing repeat sales of the same home. As far as I know, it is the best way to get a handle on the price appreciation in actual homes and condos. According to Case-Shiller, during that exuberant period from 2000 to 2006, homes appreciated at a compounded rate of 9.58 percent and delivered a total return of 89.60 percent to unleveraged owners (see Table 14-1).

But those figures don't tell us much because the *real* benefits to real estate speculators accrue from the generous amount of leverage available to buyers. I deliberately use the term *speculators* because the amount of leverage many real estate "investors" were actually using during that time frame was either outright speculation or, perhaps, pure gambling.

Table 14-1   Case-Shiller U.S. National Home Price Index

YEAR*	INDEX	% OF CHANGE	NAV 1000	% UNDERPERFORM TO T-BILL†
1987	66.18	6.69	1067	+
1988	71.22	7.62	1148	+
1989	75.37	5.83	1215	(2.54)
1990	74.59	(1.03)	1203	(8.84)
1991	74.65	0.08	1204	(5.52)
1992	74.74	0.12	1205	(3.39)
1993	75.91	1.57	1224	(1.33)
1994	77.89	2.61	1256	(1.29)
1995	79.51	2.08	1282	(3.52)
1996	81.18	2.10	1309	(3.11)
1997	84.80	4.46	1367	(0.80)
1998	90.81	7.09	1464	+
1999	98.29	8.24	1585	+
2000	107.90	9.78	1740	+
2001	116.23	7.72	1874	+
2002	128.58	10.63	2073	+
2003	142.29	10.66	2295	+
2004	163.06	14.60	2630	+
2005	*186.97*	*14.66*	*3015*	+
2006	186.44	(0.28)	3007	(5.08)
2007	170.75	(8.42)	2753	(13.08)
2008	139.41	(18.35)	2248	(19.95)
2009	136.00	(2.45)	2193	(2.55)
2010	130.38	(4.13)	2102	(4.25)

	1987–2010	2000–2010	1987–99	2000–06
CMPD Return	3.18%	2.60%	3.68%	9.58%
Inflation CMPD	2.90	2.40	3.30	2.60

Table 14-1   Case-Shiller U.S. National Home Price Index *(Continued)*

	1987–2010	*2000–2010*	*1987–99*	*2000–06*
Aver. Underperformance	(3.17)	(4.08)	(2.38)	—
Total Return	110.20	32.60	58.50	89.70
Worst Drawdown	(30.3)	(30.3)	(1.03)	—

* Case-Shiller Index began on March 31, 1987 at 62.03; therefore, only three quarters of data are available for that year.

†The plus sign (+) in the last column indicates that the index overperformed relative to T-bills for those years.

From the mid-twentieth century until quite recently a great deal of residential real estate was initially leveraged at a 5:1 ratio. It was the reciprocal of the traditional 20 percent down payment that accredited buyers were required to put up. That hefty lever was predicated on the idea that the national average of homes and apartments didn't do double-digit price retreats, and almost no one seemed to question it. Surveying the situation at the end of the twentieth century, residential real estate appeared to be a particularly safe investment. Its unleveraged AU during C/SI's nearly 13 years of existence registered a fairly low (2.38) percent, and stories about price trends from 1987 back to World War II would seem to back up that figure.

(Oh yes, "long ago," during the Depression, it was estimated that real estate did take an approximate 25 percent dive. But, egads, that was during the most horrendous time in our economic history, and the price reduction was nothing when compared to the devastation in equities and other risk assets during that time.)

It is likely that real estate's extraordinary stability was based on the fact that, until quite recently, the overwhelming majority of homes were bought to live in, rather than to rent out or flip for a profit. In the past, homes were treated more like an extended consumer durable good, and, as such, price changes for the most part reflected the rate of inflation. CSI's compounded appreciation for the years 1987 to 1999 totaled 3.68 percent, which was actually 0.38 percent over the 3.3 percent annualized rate of inflation for that period.

Yet once a significant crowd of speculators, putting up front only marginal amounts of money, were attracted to buying homes for profit opportunities, the character of the residential real estate market changed. And what happens when a speculative crowd, because of its frequent activity, attains the muscle to dominate some economic enterprise? In the words of Lord Keynes, "Speculation may do no harm as bubbles on a steady stream of enterprise. But the position is serious when enterprise becomes the bubble on a whirlpool of speculation. When the … property market [author's words] becomes a by-product of the activities of a casino, the job is likely to be ill-done."

A CHANGING REAL ESTATE MARKET

A notable change took place in the real estate market. Case-Shiller Index's hefty 9.58 percent annualized return during the sizzling 2000–2006 bull market broke away from the 2.60 percent compounded rate of inflation. It was a sign that the market for homes and apartments was taking on the coloration of an investment market, wherein volatile up-and-down fluctuations occur fairly frequently.

Prior to the early 1920s, the stock market had been a pretty tame affair, dominated by corporate owners along with long-term, dividend-seeking investors. The speculative crowd was just a bubble (lowercase) atop a steady stream of industrial progress.

According to an index constructed by the Cowles Foundation for Research in Economics, which dates back through 1871, stock market returns were considerably more stable prior to 1926 than afterwards. In that early period, dividends made up the major part, about 72 percent, of the annualized 7.2 percent return; capital appreciation alone (ex-dividends) accounted for only 28 percent. But, in the post-1926 period the numbers flipped. Capital appreciation made up approximately 56 percent of the total, while dividends accounted for about 42 percent. But most significantly, in that earlier period, the stock market's very worst drawdown on an annual basis was 21.79 percent in 1907, and only one other such drawdown breached the 20 percent marker (according to *Ibbotson's* data, which he acknowledged to be of lesser quality).

But once Edgar Lawrence Smith published his *Stocks as Long-Term Investments*[1] in the early 1920s, touting the merits of stock returns vis-à-vis bonds, a speculative crowd, trading on razor-thin margins, invaded Wall Street. The arrival of this crowd changed the complexion of that market to one in which the ups and downs became more extreme, implying stock market breaks would no longer be contained at the "just above" 20 percent level. In less than 5 years, theory became reality, as the Great Crash of 1929 began and stock prices kept falling until they had erased 64.21 percent, on an annual basis, from their 1928 closing price. Four other losses of 35 percent or more followed in the years since.

REAL ESTATE SPECULATORS IN THE 2000s

Allowing residential real estate speculators to lever at a horse and buggy 5:1 leverage ratio once a large speculative crowd took the real estate market into a volatile automobile age was equivalent to handing driver's licenses to toddlers. And if more evidence was needed that residential real estate could easily fall by much more than 20 percent, there was Exhibit A—the Japanese real estate market, which fell by 50 to 80 percent during their "lost decade," or as we now say "lost decades." Yet, these dangerous implications were ignored by the gunslinging real estate speculators.

Typically, residential real estate speculators receive a cash flow on their investment, which in most cases covers operating expenses, such as maintenance, taxes, insurance, management fees (if there are any), and at least a large portion of the mortgage costs. Normally, operating expenses total about 40 percent, or a bit more, of the property's income stream, which in turn, after an allowance for vacancies, typically totals about 10 percent of the property's value. That would leave about 6 percent of the property's worth available to cover mortgage payments.

In some cases, all of the mortgage costs would have been covered, with even a small portion left over to provide the speculator with a *positive cash flow*. But probably, in just as many cases, the real estate speculator would come up short and experience a *negative cash flow*. That means feeding the investment out of one's own pocket in hopes of future appreciation. Since, as far as I know, there are not any reliable statistics on the amount of positive to negative cash flows that real estate speculators actually had experienced, I think considering income to expenses a wash for the 5:1 speculator simplifies matters without doing much, if any, harm to the accounting outcomes. Also in the interest of clarity, mortgages are assumed to be interest-only mortgages (normally, in the early years only small portions go to pay down principal anyway) and tax ramifications are ignored. (Actually, depreciation write-offs may have been used to avoid paying taxes on any profits resulting from real estate sales.) To be fair and to even matters out, mortgage origination points and selling costs, which at a negotiated 5 percent would be a 25 percent hit—five times the 5 percent—to 5:1 levered speculators' net equity portion, are also ignored.

Table 14-2 shows an estimated outcome to residential real estate speculators levered at 5:1 ratio and then again based on a considerably more conservative 2.5:1 ratio (40 percent down payment). The 5:1 lever assumes a break-even cash flow. The 2.5:1 levered investor probably received some positive cash flow, as the mortgage payments were 25 percent less costly (based on covering only 60 percent of the property cost, as opposed to an 80 percent cover). Assume a 1.5 percent positive cash flow, which comes to one-quarter of the approximate 6 percent available for mortgage payments.

Table 14-2   Case-Shiller Leveraged at 5:1 and 2.5:1 (2000–2010)

YEAR	5:1	MORTGAGE DEBT	NAV	2.5:1	MORTGAGE DEBT	NAV
		400,000	100,000	15	150,000	100,000
2000	48.90	595,600	148,900	25.95	188,900	125,900
2001	38.60	825,600	206,400	20.80	228,100	152,100
2002	53.15	1,264,400	316,100	28.07	292,300	194,900
2003	53.30	1,938,400	484,600	28.15	374,500	249,700
2004	73.00	3,353,200	838,300	38.00	516,900	344,600
2005	73.30	5,811,200	1,452,800	38.15	714,100	476,100
2006	(1.40)	5,811,200	1,432,460	0.80	719,800	479,900
CMPD Return	+46.27			+25.11		
2007	(42.10)	5,811,200	822,540	(19.55)	719,800	386,100
2008	(91.75)	5,811,200	(394,750)	(44.38)	719,800	217,000
2009	(12.25)	5,811,200	(527,450)	(4.62)	719,800	207,000
2010	(20.65)	5,811,200	(745,670)	(8.82)	719,800	188,700
CMPD Return	(Negative)			+5.94		
WDD*	100%+			(60.68)%		

* WDD = Worst Drawdown.

Also, in both cases, we assumed "shoot-for-the-moon" speculators reinvested paper profits back into real estate each year-end at the same leverage ratio. However, when the Case-Shiller Index posts a down year, as was the case in 2007 and 2008, there are no paper profits to reinvest at year-end. We also assume no sales; when prices are retreating, property buyers back off and that market becomes very illiquid. It was quite hard to sell real estate without accepting big discounts, and property was nearly impossible to dump when the real estate market seized up after Lehman collapsed. It is, in fact, not inconceivable that more than a few of those "Wild West" speculators are still stuck with many of their properties (intentionally or not) to this day.

During the 2000–2006 real estate bull market, both 5:1 and 2.5:1 strategies made bundles of money. Unsurprisingly the 5:1

real estate speculators did better, burning up the track with an amazing compounded return of 46.27 percent, while the number for the more conservative 2.5:1 speculators was a respectable 25.11 percent. Both made for smiley-faced speculators. By December 2006, the 5:1 real estate speculators who had started with $100,000 were minted into "on-paper" millionaires and then some. In a mere 7 years, they had accumulated real estate holdings worth $7,243,700 and their equity stake had grown to $1,432,500. Of course, they were acclaimed "geniuses" by many. The total return for the conservative 2.5:1 speculators was also generous, although not nearly as spectacular, and by period's end, they were able to produce a financial statement that showed net equity of more than $479,000.

THE DARWINIAN INVESTORS IN THE WILD WEST

Meanwhile, Darwinian investors also had their own weapon, ART, to venture out into "Wild West" territory. With the lowering of restrictions on down payments opening up the market to a huge new block of salivating buyers, this could certainly be a good time to consider levering ARTs, but not to the extremes that residential real estate speculators were doing. We will adhere to the leverage guidelines we laid out in the previous chapter.

As the period began, a survey of the prior 28 years showed the cost of borrowed funds averaged about 8.50 percent, which indicated a projected average underperformance ceiling of 4.25. At a 1.5 lever, ART's projected AU clocked in at 4.39 percent, its 28-year AU of (2.71) multiplied by 162 percent, just marginally over our ceiling. Given the amount of leverage flowing into the actual physical real estate market, along with ART's 28-year compounded return of 13.10 percent, the 0.14 percent breach of the ceiling did not seem a major violation of our leverage rules. So let's allow a tiny stretch and lever it at 1.5:1. See Table 14-3.

Table 14-3   Active REIT (ART) Levered at 1.5:1

YEAR	ART 1.5:1	INT. COST T-BILL + 1.70	TOTAL	NAV 1000	DRAWDOWN
2000	+38.28	(3.80)	+34.48	1345	
2001	20.90	(2.77)	18.13	1589	
2002	4.47	(1.67	2.80	1633	
2003	55.18	(1.36)	53.82	2512	
2004	52.83	(1.45)	51.38	3803	
2005	21.19	(2.34)	18.85	4520	
2006	58.54	(3.25)	55.29	7018	
CMPD Return +32.09					
Pre–07/27	(24.95)	(1.75)	(26.70)	5144	
Post–07/27	12.26	(1.43)	10.83	5702	**(18.75)**
2008	19.67	(1.65)	18.02	6730	
2009	44.26	(0.90)	43.36	9648	
2010	42.24	(0.91)	41.33	13,636	
11-year CMPD Return +26.81					
Average Underperformance (2.12)					
Worst Drawdown (18.75)					

The 1.5:1 levered ART delivered a 32.09 percent compounded return during the 2000–2006 real estate bull market and investors racked up a total profit in excess of 600 percent. Although well below the speculative 5:1 strategy, ART did outdistance the conservative 2.5:1 speculative strategy by a good amount. Even by "Wild West" standards, it was a respectable performance, especially considering there was no need to fuss over finding, contracting for, fixing up, and maintaining actual real estate properties.

Yet by December 2006, residential real estate was in the earliest stages of what would turn out to be a more than 30 b percent retreat (so far), which would shock participants. Consequently, the three following years would not be kind to home and condo speculators.

So-called "genius" 5:1 real estate speculators, unless they had sold a decent portion of their properties pre-2008 and salted away some of the profits, were ushered into the torture chambers. By the time 2008 was over, they had given back not only all of their paper profits, but their original investment capital had evaporated as well. Adding insult to injury, they were deeply *underwater*—they owed more on their properties than they could be sold for. At the end of 2010, the original $100,000 speculators, had they not gone bankrupt, owed about $745,670 more than the properties were worth. Ouch!

Yet, let's give them a hard-to-believe "what-if" alternative (see Table 14-4). Imagine they had made the deft move of selling off half their holdings at the end of 2007; that would be $3,316,870 worth ($5,811,200 in mortgages plus equity of $822,540 divided by 2), at an optimistic 5 percent discount in a depressed, hard-to-sell real estate market. (We are sticking to our claim of not including selling commissions.) That would reduce their equity stake by $165,840 to $657,300. Had they been clever enough to sell off half their inventory in late 2007, before the gates slammed shut, they would have ended 11 years of real estate speculation in the hole at negative $88,200. Egads, they could have done better as a Walmart greeter and saved themselves from the enormous headaches they must have endured.

Table 14-4   5:1 CS Alternative: Sell One-Half in Late 2007

YEAR	CS RETURN	DEBT-FUNDED REAL ESTATE ($)	EQUITY ($)	LEVER RATIO
2007	December	5,811,200	822,540	8:1
2007*		2,494,330	656,700	4.8:1
2008	(18.35)	2,494,330	78,485	32.5:1
2009	(2.45)	2,494,330	15,450	162:1
2010	(4.13)	2,494,330	(88,200)	Negative

*After a $3,316,870 sale at a 5 percent discount totaling $165,840, which was subtracted from equity. (The $3,316,870 went to pay off mortgage debt.)

The more conservative 2.5:1 speculators fared better (see Table 14-2). By late 2010, they were still hanging on with their heads above water. But their equity stake had taken a (60.68) percent drubbing and their 380 percent profit had dwindled to a net plus of about 89 percent. The 11-year compounded return had slipped to a modest 5.94 percent, well below the S&P 500's 39-year number, albeit with a lot more actual work and woes.

Meanwhile, ART investors got a real estate sell alert in July 2007. After dumping their REITs, they would have finished 2007 off by (18.75) percent and then resumed their winning ways. (For consistency's sake, we also leveraged the intermediate Treasury note bought in July 2007 at 1.5:1.) By period's end, they had increased their starting stake by over 1263 percent, and their 11-year compounded return remained at an extraordinary 26.81 percent (see Table 14-3).

Yet, most importantly, ART investors, unlike most of the actual residential real estate speculators who were unaware of or unconcerned by the fact that any such sell signal had been given, would not have had to suffer with unsold inventory through 2008 and beyond. Their worst drawdown, on an annual basis, of (18.75) percent, was way below the huge declines real estate speculators had to sweat through.

There are, as yet, no surefire rules on how to handle real estate leverage, but we now realize something we hadn't known a few years back: residential real estate *can* fall, on a national level, by well more than 20 percent. And given that new information, I think it is safe to say that leverage rates of 5:1 (and probably 4:1 also), rebooted at fairly short intervals, are, to put it delicately, excessively risky. As we saw, 5:1 speculators went from being geniuses to becoming deep-in-the-red bag holders.

BUYING AND OCCUPYING REAL ESTATE

Owning your own home or apartment is the cornerstone of the American Dream, and the above rant about excessive leverage should not necessarily be taken to disparage buying a home or condo to actually "live in" with a 20 percent down payment. In buying real estate to "occupy," some things change. First, the home once again becomes a consumer durable and mortgage payments are made in lieu of the rent, which the owner would have had to pay anyway. Second, there is a good chance that, as long as the home has not been treated as an ATM machine, leverage drift will work to the buyer's benefit.

Suppose a family bought a $250,000 home in late December 1999, with a $50,000 down payment and a 30-year $200,000 principal-paying mortgage. By the end of 2006, they would have paid off about $15,000 of principal (based on an original 8 percent mortgage, the prevailing rate at the time of their purchase) plus their home would have appreciated by approximately 89.5 percent, valuing it at about $473,500. At that time, the home-owning family would still owe about $185,000 on their mortgage, but would have approximately $288,500 in home equity; their leverage ratio would have drifted way down from 5:1 to about 1.65:1.

During the following 4 years, the value of the house would have fallen by about 30.1 percent, indicating a worth of about $331,000 (see Table 14-5). Meanwhile, approximately another $12,500 of mortgage principal would have been paid down, leaving the balance due on the mortgage at about $173,500. That still leaves the home owner with about $157,500 of home equity. Although the home owners' stake had fallen by $131,000 or 45 percent from its December 2006 peak figure, they were still up 215 percent or $107,500 on their original $50,000 investment. And their leverage ratio would have drifted back up to a bit more than 2:1, not horrible. Besides, presumably they had a nice place to live in during that time.

Table 14-5   Three Home Buyers

	ORIGINAL			2010		
YEAR	PURCHASE PRICE	DOWN PAYMENT	MORTGAGE	HOME VALUE	MORTGAGE DEBT	OWNER EQUITY
2000	$250,000	$50,000	$200,000	$331,000	$173,500	$157,500
2006–1*	473,500	94,500	379,000	331,000	358,500	(27,500)
2006–2†	473,500	158,000	315,500	331,000	298,000	33,000

*20% down payment

†33.3% down payment

However, the story unfolds differently for the family that might have bought that $473,500 home in December 2006. It took a $94,500 (20 percent) down payment along with a 30-year $379,000 mortgage to purchase the house. In the ensuing 4 years, until the end of 2010, the new owners made approximately $20,500 in principal payments (based on a prevailing 6 percent mortgage rate), but their remaining mortgage debt of $358,500 was above the $331,000 value of their home, and that would have left them about $27,500 underwater.

The situation improves if the second family had been cautious real estate buyers, deciding to under leverage. Suppose they plunked down 33.33 percent—instead of the traditional 20 percent—or about $158,000, and took on a $315,500 mortgage. After paying down about $17,500 of principal, their mortgage debt would total about $298,000, which was still $33,000 less than their $331,000 home. They remained positive, although about $125,000 (79 percent) of their equity would have disappeared down the drain and their leverage ratio would now stand at about a towering 10:1 ratio. Yet, after allowing for another estimated $27,000 of principal repayments, they would still be able to absorb a further 18 percent fall in their home price during the following 5-year period and remain above water.

Residential real estate, in the early 2000s, rhymed with the late 1920s stock market; leverage ratios went amok. In both cases, speculators, with assumptions of risk that were way too low were operating with equity stakes of 10 to 20 percent, or less. Both then suffered enormous losses, as prices fell far more than participants had thought possible a few years earlier. It was the residential real estate market's first real shock in modern times, and like the stock market after 1929, it is in the process of finding a more appropriate level of risk and resulting leverage ratios.

In the next chapter, we discuss "who we are"—flawed agents—and see how those flaws may affect decision making.

PART 5

A DARWINIAN
WORLD

In a Darwinian world, agents are not as smart as they think they are. When dealing with an uncertain future they are, often, faulty decision makers. That is mostly due to an inner agenda, which we shall go into, while also providing some hints on how to improve our decision-making powers.

Then we will talk about the main components of a social search engine and how we can use them to evaluate the current situation. Finally, in the conclusion, I will go back to the question asked at the beginning of this book: Are investment markets beatable?

CHAPTER 15

THE AGENT ROLE IN A DARWINIAN WORLD

Good reasoning skills are supposed to be the route to wise decisions. Yet since the late 1950s, psychologists have been conducting experiments which show that *humans are really bad at reasoning.* The psychologists contend that a host of inner emotions and mental biases cloud our view of reality and keep us from objectively assessing evidence.

Early market thinkers warned about two powerful emotions—fear and greed—which had profound and detrimental effects on investors' decision making. Greed was thought of as an insatiable desire for wealth that kept feeding on itself until, finally, the god of Avarice threw a bolt of bad luck the investor's way and a good deal of the wealth disappeared. Fear, on the other hand, was described as an animal-like response to an unexpected huge loss. Typically it began as an uneasy feeling in the pit of one's belly and crept all the way up, until it froze the investor's brain. Then with much difficulty, said investor pried open his or her mouth, usually just in time, to hysterically yell "sell" quite near some important market bottom.

In the 1950s, Herbert A. Simon, a Nobel laureate and professor at Carnegie Mellon University, posed a direct challenge to the idea of (perfect) rationality. After studying real people making decisions in real companies, he claimed the role that reason played in decision making was limited. According to his new theory, rationality was "bounded" by constraints imposed by the lack of computational ability and the cost and time of obtaining information. Thus, in decision making and judgment making, people utilize experience-based "rules of thumb" that draw from their own available information, and it makes for "satisfactory," rather than optimal, solutions. The implication: Humans are smart, but not that smart.

Since then, a group of market behavioralists, drawing on psychology, studied the matter in more detail and reported a host of mental biases—from anchoring to confirmation bias—hardwired into our mental apparatus that serve as unconscious stumbling blocks to proper decision making.

Probably the most important idea was that of *cognitive dissonance*, coined by the social psychologist Leon Festinger. According to him, when our beliefs conflict with reality, most of us try to reshape reality to match our beliefs, rather than the other, more rational, way around. As an example, Festinger liked to use the Millerites, a millenarian religious sect that believed that Jesus Christ would return to earth on October 22, 1844. When Christ did not make his expected appearance on that day, many Millerites did not abandon their faith. Rather they constructed elaborate rationalizations justifying Christ's nonappearance. Some argued He had returned spiritually; others claimed the event had actually occurred in Heaven rather than on earth.

The fact is that most of us, non-Millerites, also pay attention to evidence that conforms to our suppositions and tend to filter out evidence that challenges them. When reality or facts fly in the face of deep-seated beliefs, we bend facts into pretzels to get the desired results so we can cling to our beliefs.

FAULTY DECISION MAKING

No doubt, untamed emotions along with a host of mental biases are often stumbling blocks to proper choice making, but perhaps they are not the chief culprits in faulty decision making. To begin with, in much of human activity, where accurate information is, more or less, available—such as designing, making, and selling commercial products; flying an airplane; or building a bridge—decision making is actually quite good. This high-level reasoning power comes from the fact that most people who worked their way into top choice-making positions were vetted along the way. Those who passed had mastered the necessary special information, and, for the most part, possessed excellent reasoning skills to boot. The marvelous economic strides of the past two centuries attest to that fact. Furthermore, we can assume these people wouldn't have been able to scamper up that ladder if they did not also have a "good-enough" governor on their emotional drives.

While emotional and psychological stumbling blocks may have limited, and even stymied, career opportunities for some people who otherwise had persuasive reasoning powers, they did not derail the impressive economic strides we made. In the big picture, these obstacles were nothing more than a mere irritant on the road of industrial progress.

However, when we deal with an unknown future, wherein decisions are based on incomplete and imperfect information, human flaws often mug our reasoning powers; that goes for the reasoning powers of the "boss" people as well. It is mostly in this space, where uncertainty rules, that human "rationality" seems to have failed us. Inserting highly educated people with superior reasoning skills into political and economic leadership roles has not resulted in a relatively error-free political or economic system. Nor has it enabled us to conquer games of uncertainty. It is in this matter of dealing with uncertainty where we will focus our concern about faulty decision making.

Decision Making in the 1930s

I submit the problem is more complicated than conjuring up the bogeymen of weak emotional governors and mental biases as the impediments to proper decision making. As an example, let us take a look at some of the chief deciders during the difficult

1930s. It was a horrible decade that included the most wrenching depression in modern times, along with the outbreak of the deadliest conflict in human history, World War II, which claimed an estimated 50 to 70 million lives.

Most historians, and the general public, have branded the political leaders at the helm during those two calamities as faulty or, to be more precise, *pathetic* decision makers. In the first case, President Herbert Hoover and his crowd were depicted as a group of out-of-touch knuckleheads who failed to recognize the feebleness of their remedies to an economy that was in a death spiral.

In the later instance, Neville Chamberlain and Edouard Daladier, the political leaders in England and France, the two countries most sensitive to German expansionist aims, were criticized as naïve appeasers lacking the fortitude to stand up to Adolf Hitler early on, when German military strength was only a pittance of what it was soon to become. Chamberlain and Daladier were faulted for not realizing that in giving in to Hitler they only whetted his expansionist appetite, thereby setting the stage for a military conflict of monstrous proportions.

In both cases, later observers often seem oblivious to the fact that they had a huge information advantage over the prior deciders. Historians and public observers knew the horrific outcomes that resulted from the earlier choices, while the choice makers, not being clairvoyant, were obviously denied that information in regard to the oncoming crises of economic hardships and Hitler's intentions prior to World War II. This information link between decision and bad outcome, available only to later observers, is called *outcome bias* (or sometimes *hindsight bias*). Yet to participants who didn't share in the advantage of hindsight, and had to deal with alternative possibilities and decision-blocking constraints that have since faded into the fog of time, the outcomes of their actions certainly didn't seem so inevitable.

I'm not so sure I know who the guilty parties were: the faulty decision-making political leaders or the later-outcome, biased judgment renderers? As you can see, the situation is a bit complicated. Perhaps we can get a fuller understanding of the problem by switching gears and taking a look at *the agent role in a Darwinian world*, in particular, how and why we agents attach to a living system.

The Big Narrative

Systems that offer a "raison d'être," or a reason for existence, as their narrative are the most elaborate of all living systems and operate at the highest level of human activity. Their offer of a reason for being is able to attract agents to link to them, as a matter of faith, because of its ability to satisfy deep human appetites.

Creating and acquiring wealth so as to improve our material life here on earth is the most prominent goal, or aspiration, of most Americans. This economic growth imperative is the narrative—the implied, unarticulated creed of our system—which feeds directly into "the American Dream." When the system is in trouble, the narrative undergoes a slight change to a repair-and-rebuild mode, which is usually a way to seek fairer ways of distributing and managing that wealth.

This system offer of economic growth and wealth creation as our modern reason for being won out over competing narratives. Perhaps the most important earlier reason for existence was salvation, as formed around religion and its code of conduct, playing an important role in the socializing (taming) process. Although essentially dethroned by the current system, religion still plays a supplementary role—living a decent, moral life—in our present system. For some, this nonconflicting aspiration is actually their chief life goal. Nonetheless, by providing an alternative lifestyle choice, this religious subsystem (along with others) adds to the system's overall richness.

High-level systems have powerful arousal techniques to shape (or if you prefer, seduce) agent aspirations and behavior to conform to system purposes. Turn on your TV or go to the movies and chances are you will soon see sumptuous homes and apartments, sleek luxurious cars, and beautiful people dressed in designer clothes jetting off to glamorous destinations, while prefeminized females throw themselves at "high-status" males, who are deemed system "heroes." Yet, you don't have to aspire to "hero-ship"; you can merely move up the ladder of material success (implying easier access to needed scarce resources) to gain social respect, along with greater choices of reproductive partners, more or less, proportionately to the material gains.

In our society, the purchase of a new home (provided it is the first or a somewhat better home than a previous one) is celebrated by a visit from friends and family members toting a bottle of wine or flowers as an acknowledgment after a guided tour of the new mini-castle that the purchaser has indeed moved up the social ladder. These system siren songs, and many more, glorifying the good, material life are the arousal signals beeped out as part of the self-organizing process to manipulate agent aspirations and bend their goals to conform to those of the system. And the message has been well received, as agents today aspire to get higher-paying jobs, nicer homes, and increased status, or create conditions so that their children will become better able to benefit from the fruits of the American Dream.

We are agents tethered to an elaborate living system, which serves as an invisible structure, much like fish trapped in a bowl. We live within the boundaries the system sets, we talk to each other in its aspiration-laden language, we abide by its code of conduct, and we adopt the roles it has created. Like it or not, we are attached to the system and connect with others via our shared belief in it. Even refuseniks are linked, as they usually define themselves by what they reject.

When we attach to the system, we link "fates." Most of us become willing to crawl over broken glass to do our part, big or little, in supporting or defending the system; this is our Darwinian agent role.

These systems, though, are in constant flux; they change with a rhythm that alternates between vigor, feeding on robust energy sources, and apathy, when energy sources diminish. Agents create a zeitgeist, a spirit of the times, to match that rhythm. These social moods operate much like a belief in which people disregard evidence conflicting with the sentiment of the day and enshrine confirming examples as object lessons in how to proceed. With this in mind, let's return to those incompetent political leaders of the 1930s and take another look at their decision-making prowess.

Revisiting the 1930s Decision Making

The prosperity and great bull market of the 1920s blinded politicians to the possibility that the economy and the stock market might be vulnerable to a serious falloff. In the spirit of those vigorous times, we were on a one-way road to a society in which "everyone would soon be bathed in riches." So when the shakeout began, politicians were reminded that predecessor public officials had navigated an economic falloff in 1920, which had briefly reached depression territory, with basically a hands-off policy. However, in that case, the economy quickly recovered from that falloff without creating much human anguish.

The benign outcome of the short post–World War I depression undoubtedly supported the general assumption that the 1930 economic falloff did not require an extraordinary government response—at least until the economy was well into an irreversible death spiral. President Hoover easily rejected advice from 1000 economists urging him not to sign the duty-raising Smoot-Hawley Tariff Act because he was well aware that in 1922, while the economy was still smoldering from the effects of the early 1920s slump, a Republican administration had raised tariffs which appeared to have helped the recovery process.

Also in the 1930s, European statesmen were still in shock from the devastation suffered in lost lives and treasures during World War I. Given the terrible outcome of the "war to end all wars"—4 horrendous years of trench warfare with a death toll estimated at about 16 million—European political leaders had no stomach for a repeat conflict with the Central Powers. Rather, in the zeitgeist of the apathetic late-1930s, the European political leaders were on the lookout for *any* excuse to duck a resumption of hostilities.

Luckily, academics and political officials had rethought the decisions preceding the prior outbreak of hostilities and concluded that the English and French had been too hasty in entering that bloody contest, World War I. Not enough consideration had been given to making accommodations, such as appeasing the Central Powers, which perhaps might have forestalled hostilities. This *reinterpretation* of the decisions preceding World War I naturally played directly into the hands of the leaders of the Allied nations, making them even more reluctant to challenge the Nazis early on. In both cases, a previous experience was interpreted by decision makers, as well as the general public at the time, as evidence to act in the way they were already predisposed to behave.

It is easy to question the political wisdom of the politicians and statesmen of the 1930s, smugly thinking we are smarter than they are. Yet they were merely dancing to the music the "mood" band of that era was playing. Had they not, they would have become political toast. Within the context of those times, how could we, absent knowledge of the outcomes, be so sure we would have decided any differently?

THE MAIN OBSTACLE: AN INNER AGENDA

In attaching to a system, or a crowd, there is a subtle and unconscious shift in personal strategy. Agents relinquish their individuality in order to keep in step with the mood of the times. They, in reality, are playing in a different game than "rational" Newtonians assume. When the future is uncertain, much of what is claimed to be faulty decision making may really be a response to an inner agenda to remain in social harmony with our crowd. And, by Darwinian rules, this may, in fact, be perfectly rational.

Nonetheless, choosing crowd approval over our rational self-interest often leads to lousy decision making. When it comes to games with sketchy information we, humans, are flawed decision makers. How then can we, flawed agents, make more rational decisions in games of uncertainty? It may not be easy, but there are several things we can try.

First: Our Knowledge Is Limited

Almost 2500 years ago, the Greek philosopher Socrates laid the foundation stone for all future knowledge seekers in his famous paradoxical phrase "… in knowing that you know nothing … you are the smartest of all." It was a warning that any one person's knowledge is limited.

Accordingly, although we may be smart, we aren't *that* smart. When we deal in matters where outcomes aren't confidently known, our faith in our ability to reason is often way overblown and we invariably know less than we think we do. We grasp at fragments of information, or pieces of knowledge, without recognizing the limited nature of those bits and pieces and how they fit into the larger puzzle of knowledge. Information is only helpful if we can make sense out of it; otherwise it is apt to seduce us into thinking we know something that we really don't. In short, in games wherein information is imperfect, we should be mindful of the limitations of our own brainpower, à la Socrates or Warren Buffett, and not take our own opinions too seriously.

Mr. Arrogant and the Cab Driver. Here is a true story about a guy who thought he knew more than he actually did. In the late 1950s, there was a smart University of Chicago (U. of C.) student, who, unlike his friends, also college students enrolled in good law and medical schools, was an avid reader of the *New York Times*. He was also a bit arrogant about what he presumed he knew.

One fine summer night, "Mr. Arrogant" and his buddies were out on the town, in their ritual Saturday night search for lively female companionship in Chicago's Rush Street district. Per usual, they weren't very lucky, but then the U. of C. guy spotted a little group marching around carrying signs in support of Fidel Castro, who at the time was operating as an insurgent guerrilla leader in the rugged Sierra Maestra Mountains of Cuba. He quickly explained to his friends that Herbert Matthews, a respected correspondent for the *New York Times*, had been singing the praises of Castro as an unflawed romantic hero—an idealistic pro-democracy rebel trying to overthrow the corrupt Batista regime and bring needed social reform to that backward country. Soon the U. of C. guy and his buddies were marching alongside the pro-Castroites, carrying signs and shouting out slogans.

His little group was having a grand time strutting around Rush Street, when all of the sudden a cab pulled up alongside and a "beefy" driver with tattoos covering his arms leans out the open window of his cab and, referring to Castro, shouts, "Damn communist!" Smart guy's student friends were taken aback, wondering if they had been had. But "Mr. Arrogant" confidently reassured them that surely a "stupid" cab driver did not know more than a top U. of C. student. He told them they could rest assured that, according to Herbert Matthews, Castro was not a communist. His friends accepted that little pep talk and resumed their public march. But naturally several years later, after Castro took over as the head of the Cuban government, he outted himself as a ... "communist."

That guy in the story was me. No, no, not the prescient, beefy, tattooed cabdriver, but rather the naive arrogant U. of C. student. Over the years, I've told this story to many people to make a point of how little we all know—especially those of us who, like me, think they are so smart. The cab driver, I presume, was not a college student, nor most likely did he bother reading the *New York Times*. Yet he knew something Mr. Smarty Pants didn't know; he knew that Castro was indeed a communist.

I'm not sure how he got that right, but the fact is that when our knowledge is not precise, getting it "right" is NOT necessarily a matter of having acquired a top "pretentious" education. Uneducated people, without any special status, often are the ones who get it "right." Yet my listeners always think my march for Castro is a cute little anecdote … but none of them get the point "right."

This story is an excellent example of how a couple of guys, relying on little bits of information, thought they knew more than they actually did. To begin, I was overly impressed by Matthews's credentials as an award-winning journalist at the *New York Times*, the national "Newspaper of Record," and I assumed him to be a responsible information gatherer. But I did not have a good enough reason to do so. I failed the test of making my information meaningful.

As for Matthews, it appears he was sleeping at the switch. There was much about Castro's background that either the reporter did not bother to find out about or, if he did, he didn't inform his readers of. Actually, Castro's checkered past included several incidents that indicated he was not a pro-democracy reformer. Most troubling were suggestions that, in his student days, as early as 1943, he had been linked to the Soviet agent in charge of recruiting Cuban youth for the U.S.S.R. Throw in allegations that "Mr. Romantic Hero" carried out two political assassinations in 1948. In one case, several witnesses identified Castro as the hit man. None of this was researched or thought relevant by a reporter who posed as a "serious" journalist.

Then finally, there is the cab driver; probably he too hadn't sought out all of the relevant information, but relied on what behaviorists call *availability* or *familiarity bias*. This bias is the information-processing shortcut of selecting the example that is most memorable or easiest to recall, in this case, probably something like radical antigovernment insurgent equals communist. Yet some of those mental shortcuts work better than buying into only one part of a story—it certainly did so in this case.

Templeton: Knowing What You Don't Know. Here is another story demonstrating our limited knowledge. This one, however, is about a guy who *knew* what he didn't know. Back in 1939, the legendary investor John Templeton, who was just getting his feet wet in the investment arena, calculated the outbreak of war in Europe would kick America out of the depression. He borrowed $10,000, called his broker, and instructed him to buy 100 shares of each of the 104 shares selling for $1 or less on the New York Stock Exchange. Shortly thereafter the broker called back to report he had done so, except for 37 companies that obviously were not worthwhile, as they were in bankruptcy proceedings. Coolly, Templeton reminded the broker that his order had been to purchase each and every stock selling for under $1, and told him to report back when he had complied with those instructions. The broker did so.

Five years later, Templeton sold all of his shares of the 104 stocks for about a $50,000 profit. And when totaling his profits, he noted that the giant share of the winnings were from the 37 bankrupt companies. Actually, companies on the brink of failure are usually the ones that show the most stunning gains when the general economy pulls out of a slump.

Templeton felt comfortable in his assessment that a war-induced resurgence in the American economy would restore corporate profitability. But, more importantly, he recognized that piece of knowledge was limited—it did not indicate which companies would be the beneficiaries. But his way around that missing piece was to include them all. The knowledge that he was not able to pick the "winners," which his broker lacked, turned what would have been a modest profit into a major (500 percent) killing.

Second: Process, Not Outcome

Retrain your mind to think process, rather than outcome. Sometimes proper decisions lead to bad outcomes. Take, as an example, a surgeon recommending a life-extending and enhancing operation, which has a 97 percent success rate, to someone in a debilitated state with only a slight chance of living for much more than a year. Even though the operation fails in 3 percent of the cases, it was the correct recommendation. But the judgment of the families of the unlucky 3 percent will, most likely, be colored by their dire outcome. They are quite likely to become critical Monday-morning quarterbacks. A decision should not be evaluated on its outcome (there are even times when a better-than-expected outcome follows a faulty decision), but rather on its thoughtfulness in relation to the information available at the time it was made (including its surmised chances for success). The real question is: Was the decider's process correct?

Third: Detach!

Plug your ears with wax so you can tune out the seductive siren songs of our system and the constant, usually meaningless, chatter from fellow members of the crowd. In doing so, you may reclaim your individuality and redirect your focus to a simple one-dimensional objective and how to get there.

To be clear, detaching doesn't mean dropping out, "hippie-style," but engaging the world only on your own terms. Detaching means selecting which arousal signals you will respond to, which emotions you will allow to gurgle to the surface, and how committed you will be to the crowd or even the zeitgeist of the times. It means gaining control of your own life, and going it alone in some areas as an adaptive "lone ranger," rather than being an unwitting marionette in a grand drama.

Fourth: Remember We Are Error-Prone Animals

Recognize we are evolutionary "trial-and-error" creatures, which means we are error-prone animals. But there are several things we can do about it.

- When an error occurs, correct it immediately.
- Don't let any important mistake go to waste by not treating it as a learning experience. Remember your errors so as to make them nonrepeatable.
- Don't view proper decision making as an all or nothing proposition. Consider the wise words of General Napoleon Bonaparte, who when talking about errors in military strategy stated, "you only have to make less of them than your opponent does." I think the same attitude can be taken toward faulty decision making. "You only have to make less of them than most others." Just as Napoleon clearly saw his objective was to "win the war," yours is to reach the finish line ahead of your benchmark. And don't forget that.
- Build imperfection into your strategy, leaving ample margins for error so as to absorb some mistakes, which you will surely make.

DETECTING THE TREND

If you are going to play in an uncertain game, keep in mind you don't have to know everything. You just have to tune out the insistent chatter and focus on one or a couple of important things that matter.

Probably the single most important factor in making more rational decisions is detecting a viable trend early on, as it provides us with the most significant piece of knowledge obtainable in times of uncertainty, which is the direction of the spinning feedback loops.

The next chapter describes some of the major attributes of a living system that you should be aware of.

CHAPTER 16

How The Major Components Of Search Engines Apply in Today's World

There is a fitness function which operates in investments, just as it does in evolution. I think we can understand investment markets better if we view them as social search engines, which attempt to find a "good-enough" narrative to "fit" a new emerging reality.

THE COMPONENTS OF THE SOCIAL SEARCH ENGINE REVIEW

Let's review how the major components of these search engines work.

Trends

Living systems move in trends—short, long, and extra-long term (smaller ones are often embedded within the larger trends)—which once begun take on a life of their own, setting a self-organizing system into motion. Trends are an exercise in crowd behavior: people respond to a message of economic and financial pain or pleasure and then spontaneously rearrange themselves and adapt—similar to a flock of birds that takes to the air in a trend-like pattern. When that motion is pointing in a forward direction, the system operates by absorbing its own forms of energy—technological innovation and new recruits are the most powerful—which allows the feedback loops to spin, directing agent behavior in a more or less consistent direction. The necessity to maintain the forward motion is internalized into the breasts of the component agents, which provides the system with its own "survival" instinct.

The Narrative

The binding glue that connects agents to the system is the *animating narrative*. It is the coherent story which identifies the system by explaining or describing an emerging new reality that resonates throughout the agent population, correlating to the behavioral changes already taking form.

However, not all stories resonate with the public. Those narratives unconnected to what is occurring on the ground—that is, the evidence provided by the direction of the actual behavioral changes—have very low batting averages as to becoming animating narratives. Instead, they are *anticipatory narratives*, or opinions, of what a group of participants think or guess is likely to happen. But humans are lousy at anticipating fundamental changes in reality without the benefit of some relevant metric, such as a trend. They are no more accurate than a flip of the coin; probably less so, because they would be fighting the prevailing behavioral pattern.

One incredibly powerful long-term narrative is the Industrial Revolution, which evolved into transportation and then information revolutions, thereby creating vast investment opportunities, along with improving living standards. The Industrial Revolution has become the accepted explanation for the enormous economic strides that have taken place in Western societies since the nineteenth century and, now, throughout the world. This narrative also indicates that even more prosperity is yet to come as people from around the globe are absorbed into a worldwide wealth-generating system. And, to be sure, it is the narrative driving Jeremy Siegel's buy-and-hold equity strategy.

However, this system path, or trend, has not been a particularly safe one; along the way, lurking behind trees and boulders, were many trolls and dragons. Those scary demons are the system threats (the anticipatory narratives) that pop up from time to time to frighten us agents and cause some of us to quit the march down the path. During the past 50 years, our wealth-generating system has encountered many threats, a few of which stand out. One such threat was a looming food shortage, which Paul Ehrlich,[1] an eminent and highly regarded Professor of Population Studies at Stanford University, alerted us to in the late 1960s. He claimed the world had run out of food resources to feed its growing population and wrote, "The battle to feed humanity is over. ... In the 1970s the world will experience starvation of tragic proportions and hundreds of millions of people will starve to death." The prestigious Club of Rome think tank soon chimed in with an enthusiastic "Amen!" Their pessimistic *Limits to Growth*, based on a computer model developed by MIT professor Jay Forrester, sold 12 million copies, to become the best-selling environmental book in world history.

In the 1970s, there was a great inflation that many thought was unstoppable, along with a problem of humongous bank loans to Latin American nations, which could not be repaid. In the late 1980s, Americans dealt with a Savings and Loan (S&L) crisis, which threatened to bring down that important financier of homes and office buildings. In the 1990s, the hand-wringing turned to government deficits, which were bleeding red ink that threatened to drown us.

Then there has been a festering entitlement problem, wherein we may have saddled our grandkids with government promises that will eat up monumental proportions of our future gross domestic product. And this is not to mention a "possible" global warming threat that politicians and newscasters still talk of daily. Keep in mind, these earlier scares, along with many others of a lesser nature, appeared intractable to many during their day.

Actually, the anticipatory narrative, or story, plays an important and generally overlooked role. During a systems trajectory, its various parts are continually moving in and out of alignment.

In calling attention to some imbalance—and potential system weakness—the anticipators challenge the dominant narrative. An open-ended conversation between the two competing narratives follows, which provides the necessary tension to keep the various parts in a "solar system–like" balance. System defenders are awakened from a slumber and attempt to remedy weaknesses, while the progression of the animating narrative is slowed, allowing time for lagging parts to catch up.

All in all, by not letting stock prices get too far ahead of an economy's underlying earning power, or spending to get either way out in front of or way behind incomes, or inventories to become either too great or too lean in relation to current sales, along with a host of other relationships, the challenging story's role is to play the devil's advocate, motivating the dominant narrative to clean up its act. The result is usually a refreshed, animating narrative that makes it become more robust. As for the anticipatory narrative, it has done its job of realigning the system, and with no further Darwinian need for it, the challenging story soon loses its energy and fades away.

Error-Prone Agents

Now, let's add in the "not that smart" error-prone agents, you and I, who play out our Darwinian roles.

When a system is in motion, there are a plethora of errors (toxins) which are the by-product of human endeavor—people make mistakes. Yet, as long as the energy sources are plentiful, the system is able to override them; a growing economy masks many mistakes. Some will fizzle out, some will be disarmed, while others will be repaired. We rolled along during the 50 years preceding 2007 rather seamlessly, albeit with two bumps on the stock market road: 1973–1974 and 2000–2002.

A Green Revolution undercut Paul Ehrlich's thesis, along with his reputation. Brady bonds ameliorated the South American loan problem. The Fed, led by Paul Volcker, teamed up with Reaganomics to wilt the great inflation. A Resolution Trust

Authority repaired the S&L crisis. Bill Clinton, with an assist from a new Republican "Contract with America" Congress, put an end to the flow of government red ink—for a bunch of years.

Consequently, a majority of agents acquire a "faith" in the system's inevitability to overcome most any obstacle and do not pay much attention to the worrywarts. Actually, such a strategy is not a bad one. If we dared try and remedy each and every error, the precious energy needed to propel the system forward would dissipate into a slew of random distractions, putting the system's forward motion in jeopardy. Besides, we are unable to recognize, before the fact, the real Cassandra from the numerous imposters.

Listen to Alan Greenspan, defending himself in late October 2008 before a congressional committee questioning his culpability in the housing bubble. In answer to why he didn't anticipate the housing collapse, he claimed that the Federal Reserve with its legions of Ph.D economists "… (was) wrong quite a good deal of the time." He went on, "… we're not smart enough as people. We just cannot see events that far in advance." Asked why he didn't heed the 2000 warning from the late Fed governor Edward Gramlich about potential problems in lending practices, Greenspan replied, "There are always a lot of people raising issues, and half the time they're wrong. The question is what do you do?"

Misperception of Risk

A general, systemwide misperception of risk is the "unavoidable error," occurring when too many people have crowded into one of the two behavioral patterns (such as risk taking or risk avoiding). Unfortunately, trends do not know when they have stretched too far. Trends draw their energy not from individuals making precise calculations of profit potential to risk but from agents flocking into a growing crowd because of a common, but unconscious, psychological attitude toward risk. And that same energy keeps them trying to scale ever higher wealth barriers, until they meet up with a particularly lethal toxin the system cannot live with. But, and this is important, the agent components don't have a clue, nor the smarts to know, how to separate that particular poisonous chaff from numerous wheat grains of transitory errors or threats. Though part of the reason that agents lack this capability is that they are looking in the wrong places.

As the crowd grows, its "faith" in the system's inevitability to overcome most any obstacle graduates into a belief that certainty has dethroned uncertainty. The number of challengers thins out and a consensus forms, perhaps around the idea that "terrible bear markets will be no more," and shouts down the few remaining differences of opinion.

The result is that assumptions about the future become unrealistically rosy and the odds for faulty business, investment, and consumption decisions shoot way up. A multitude of economic problems develop. We try to fix one and then another; we begin thinking if we can do so then the machine will be able to operate flawlessly once again. But that's not much help because they were merely symptoms ... the wrong place to look. The true "unavoidable error" is a general misperception of risk.

Fluctuation

The necessity to clear the system of its embedded errors guarantees fluctuation. This brings us to an important law of systems; that is, to ensure their own future systems must flush out most of those embedded toxins, including those gullible gamblers who donned the disguise of investors. If this sounds a bit like a bathroom call, it is similar. In economics and investing terms, these bathroom calls are nasty recessions and big, grizzly bear markets that disgorge our hard-earned savings. Living systems need them, from time to time, to eliminate the accumulation of waste by-products so as to ensure their long-term viability.

Although errors are an integral part of the system wiring, it doesn't mean we shouldn't try to find those that did us in and attempt to fix them. That hunt is not totally in vain. Although the search for them will not allow us to make the system crisis-proof, it does play an important part in making a system more robust and enabling it to achieve a higher level of efficiency, though not so much so that it doesn't still need some potty stops.

A description of the components of social systems is a saga of a forced agent adaption, under conditions of uncertainty, imposed by the market, place through its price mechanism. In a world that is constantly in motion, living systems must foster adaptive changes in their participating agents' behavior; in the economic and finan-cial sphere that means going from a cautious risk-avoiding mode to animal-spirited and risk-taking behavior, and back again. If agents fail to do so, system survival is put in jeopardy.

"REAL STOCK" MARKET BUBBLES

As of late March 2011, it appears we are in the early stages of another forced agent adaptive march, so let us try to size up the situation through a CAS lens. To begin with, an enormous "bubble" popped in 2008. The popping of a genuine bubble is perhaps the most potent wealth destroyer we know of, usually fol-lowed by a decade or more of economic pain and agent hardship. Just ask Carmen Reinhardt and Kenneth Rogoff, authors of *This Time Is Different*, which chronicled eight centuries of breaking bubbles and their aftermath.[2]

Bubbles, however, are actually fairly rare; in the past 90 years, there have been only two *real* stock market bubbles in the United States, and there was also one in Japan for good measure. Yet, bubbles, as we have said, do not come out of nowhere; they are the result of a society-wide misperception of risk, which leads to a mass delusion, reinforced by rapidly rising prices that dis-credits the few skeptics that warn of trouble.

Working Definition

To get a clearer picture of what constitutes a "real" bubble, I am going to propose a simple working definition of a stock market bubble to distinguish it from the rash of imposters.

Take a look at Figure 16-1. We can assume a "real" bubble has formed when a market index price, after reaching a new 20-year (or more) high (that tells us a psychology of "low risk" has probably locked in), then triples from that level within the following 5-year period. This parabolic rise provides *prima facie* evidence that the trend has broken free from its solarlike path, and acquired a host of unsustainable imbalances.

This is because with so many believing in the dominant narrative there is no viable challenging narrative to play a restraining role. Without this restraint, the animating story runs amuck; investors might become willing to pay "pie in the sky" prices to own money-losing dot-com stocks, or a gullible public, with inadequate up-front money, may begin buying real estate based on nothing more than a hope and a prayer for some future appreciation. Valuations, in all likelihood, will have pulled far away from their supporting components or the so-called "underlying fundamentals" indicating that cracks are opening up under our feet. The chance of something that we did not expect going very wrong (say, a Lehman Brothers type bankruptcy) increases exponentially.

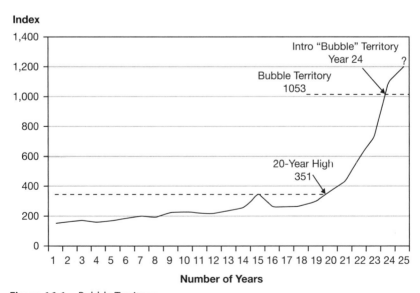

Figure 16-1   Bubble Territory

The Bubble of the 1920s

The Dow Jones Industrial Average closed at 365.20 on August 19, 1929, which was triple its 20-year high closing price of December 31, 1924, of 120.51 (see Figure 16-2).

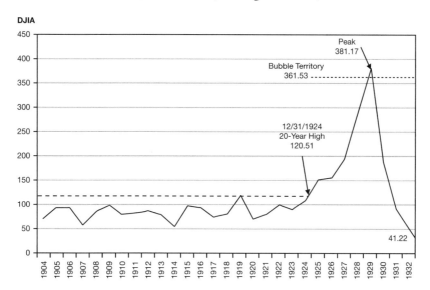

Figure 16-2   Dow Jones Industrial Average, 1904–1932

Two weeks later, the bubble peaked with the Dow at 381.17, just over 4 percent into bubble territory. Afterwards, it fell to 41.22, or 88.7 percent beneath bubble territory.

Japan's Bubble of the 1980s

On April 22, 1987, the Nikkei 225 closed at 24,097, which was three times its 20-year high closing price of 8,020 on December 6, 1982 (see Figure 16-3).

But it took another 2²⁄₃ years, with an additional rise of 61.5 percent, before the peak was reached on December 29, 1989, at 38,915. Since then it has fallen as low as 7,054, which was 70.7 percent below its first bubble sighting. Moreover, since mid-November 1991, it has not been in bubble territory for even a

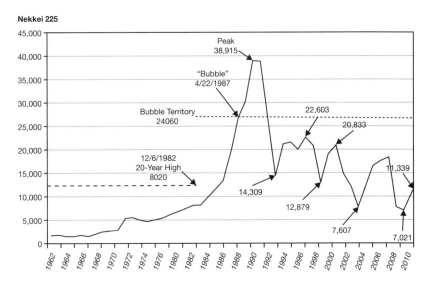

Figure 16-3   Nekkei 225, 1967–2010

single day. And when last seen, March 31, 2011, nearly 24 years after first reaching bubble territory, it was trading at 9,755, still 59.5 percent below its entry into the nosebleed level.

The Double Bubble

The most recent bubble actually began on December 23, 1999, when the S&P 500 closed at 1458.34, which was more than three times its February 15, 1995, 20-year high, closing price of 484.54 (see Figure 16-4).

A peak occurred 4 months later at 1527.46, which was not quite 5 percent higher. After falling 49 percent, the market recovered to register a second peak on October 9, 2007, at 1565.15, which was a tad higher than the earlier one. Since then, prices have fallen to 676, or about 53.5 percent below its first venture into bubble territory. As of March 31, 2011, after a vigorous stock market rally, the S&P 500 was still almost 10 percent below bubble territory.

Although this bubble-identifying formula is quite likely to bend somewhat in the future, it may still be able to serve as a rough guide to recognize future bubbles. We can note the bubbles have

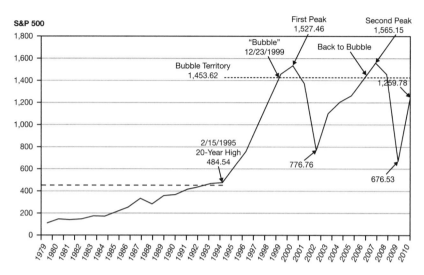

Figure 16-4   S&P 500, 1979–2010

gotten progressively longer (the last one took 7 years and almost 10 months to reach its peak), indicating a government learning curve on how to delay its destructive effects. On the flip side of the coin, this tentative formula may help dismiss some of the more naive ideas of a bubble, those that are not likely to be followed by anywhere near a decade of wealth destruction.

Right now, we are facing the aftermath of a "double" bubble. The massive and nearly simultaneous collapse in both the real estate and stock markets—from late 2006 (in real estate) to early 2009—unleashed a gigantic destructive economic force that has had a sobering effect on agent psychology, setting off a major shift to a cautious, risk-avoiding behavioral mode. Agents are in the process of deleveraging and repairing their personal balance sheets, which had gotten way out of line, and that, usually, takes some time. Given the enormity of the bubble age and the gigantic misallocations created, including a massive expansion in consumption built on the back of a mile-high mountain of debt (both private and public), this behavioral shift seems quite appropriate. And we still appear to be well short of achieving a societywide cautious and risk-avoiding mind-set. If the new economic reality is as ominous as it appears to many, including myself, it certainly seems that the system has to finish the job of herding us agents into the proper behavioral response. That means that over the next several years or more, there will be too many feedback loops spinning in a downward direction.

But there is another side to this story. A good deal of the economic resources that large parts of the population have come to feel entitled to were placed out of their reach during the 2008–09 collapse. That isn't all; while suffering through enormous downshifts in lifestyle, the same group witnessed many top "fat cats" who had also made some terrible decisions being bailed out to the tune of billions of dollars. This disconnection between actions and consequences seems grossly unfair and angers many. Our politicians can't take those sentiments lightly, as disgruntled agents have a potent weapon, the vote, and if angry enough could use it unwisely.

THE POLITICIANS' ROLE

This brings us to the role of the politicians. They, quite rightly, recognize if the economic ship isn't righted fairly quickly, they will become an endangered species. They are also aware of the fact that they have some weapons—Keynesian stimulus or deep tax cuts—which could be fairly potent and used in an attempt to get our economy back onto a growth-minded track. On the other hand, there is huge disagreement between the two parties as to which of the presumed potent weapons is the proper one to use.

Yet, if either of the activist approaches were to work, it would encourage a repetition of spending patterns that had already become excessive, forestalling the natural adaptive response to the debacle that had occurred, and that's extremely dangerous. If the much-needed adaptive response is blocked and the agent population does not become much more cautious and subdued, we could experience some monstrous unintended consequences which could, perhaps, loosen our system from its centuries' old moorings. That would put our system in grave danger of morphing into something we are not prepared for, or perhaps even system failure.

The next decade or so is likely to feature a mighty wrestling match between agents in the private sector, attempting to complete their adaption to a new dismal economic reality, and a frustrated government, fighting that response in a desperate attempt to restart our economic engine in hopes of lifting us out of this dark hole; the outcome depends on who gains the upper hand. In terms of complex adaptive systems, the system is going on a search for the narrative that best explains the emerging new political-economic structure. If the agents prevail, as they have in the past, the picture going forward is likely to resemble Japan during its post-1990 "lost decades" with government attempts to re-stimulate the economy providing the fodder for some vigorous rallies, or mini-bulls, which soon run smack into a brick wall—stagflation.

Should the government gain the upper hand, which is not inconceivable, it could be on the back of a mind-boggling inflation or something else resembling a controlled, "quasi" socialism. And, as the battle rages, it would behoove investors to pay attention to the shifting direction of the feedback loops.

CHAPTER 17

CONCLUSION: DON'T SELL EVOLUTION SHORT

I started this book with the intention of giving it my best. I introduced two investment tools based on Darwinian concepts. The first tool was the notion that variation can work for investors just about as well as it does for evolution. I constructed a passive buy-and hold investment strategy based on four negatively cor-related, major pillars of our wealth-generating system and beat the S&P 500, B&H return while also sporting a much lower risk profile.

The second tool I introduced was a 1-year/6-month algo-rithm—based on finding the critical levels that complex adaptive systems proponents talk about—to take those four asset classes active. This approach proved quite successful in the stock, real estate, gold, and long-term Treasuries markets. Risk/reward ratios beat their passive counterparts by "bragging" amounts. Then I levered that active strategy up and generated returns that were positively mouthwatering, while retaining benign risk characteristics.

A recent example of the algorithm in action: in the first half of 2009, following the most staggering financial collapse since the 1930s, a dark cloud of fear hung over the investment landscape. Many, if not most, respected market commentators were still look-ing for lower, perhaps much lower, stock prices. A smaller band of market pundits, however, thought we had turned a corner and a better economy and a higher stock market were on their way (though many in this latter camp had been repeating that mantra since the summer of 2008). As per usual, both sides presented ample evidence to make their case, leaving most investors still in a fog of confusion. So, how do we decide?

Making a decision wasn't hard for followers of the Darwinian algorithm. On June 1, 2009, less than 3 months after the stock market's March bottom, the S&P 500 made a 6-month high, providing B&S investors—who by the way had sidestepped the 2008–2009 bear market—with the all-clear sign to buy stocks. The S&P 500 finished that day at 942.87. As of the end of March 2011, the S&P 500 was 44 percent higher (including dividends). Furthermore, in late fall 2010, the National Bureau of Economic Research (the official business cycle arbiter) reported that the Great Recession, which had begun in December 2007, had indeed officially ended in June 2009, coincidently just about the time our buy signal was rendered.

It was not until late 2010 that we could fully appreciate all the information embedded in that buy signal. Though hard to believe at the time, it was telling us:

- The bear stock market was over.
- The economic recession was about spent.
- Some sort of an economic recovery, along with rallying stock prices, had just begun.

Bulls-eye!

How many of the numerous economic and stock market models had both evaded the 2008–09 bear market and imparted that same information in early 2009?

DON'T FORGET—NOTHING LASTS

As discussed earlier, in a Darwinian world, nothing lasts, and if this book is successful enough to reach a decent-sized audience, that could well be the fate of this algorithm. In revealing the algorithm, I may very well have pulled the carpet out from beneath its feet.

Any investment formula that attracts too many followers will no longer work. There is no, and cannot be any, investment method that posits superior, market-beating returns that can be passed on to nearly "all" investors. We cannot all be winners in the investment game. If any such convincing strategy was revealed, most investors would buy when the Holy Grail told them to and sell when the formula said to dump. Who then would be the people they buy from or sell to?

Keep in mind, any crowd of publicly revealed algorithm followers telegraphs its moves. It therefore doesn't take much for a new parasitic minority crowd to form with the sole purpose of feeding off the formula followers. Their modus operandi is purchasing when the market nears an algorithm buy point, continuing to do so until they have pushed the market through the point, and then unloading on the bulge created when fans of the algorithm buy in. A lot of the algorithm signals would become false, and formula groupies could become toast.

Something somewhat similar happened following the publication of two well-received investment books, both of which attracted the public's attention by revealing evidence that long-term stock market investors had reaped handsome returns during prior periods. The first book, by Edgar Allen Smith (*Stocks as Long Term Investments*), was published in 1924. The second book, by Jeremy Siegel (*Stocks for the Long Run: The Definitive Guide to Financial Market Returns & Long-Term Investment Strategies*), was released in 1994. In both cases, after about a 5-year stock market run-up, no doubt partially attributable to each book's message, the stock market reached a peak and then experienced a decade of falling prices. Stocks suffered a compounded loss of (0.9) percent from 1929 to 1938. Then from 1999 to 2008, equities registered another compounded loss of (1.4) percent. These losses were the two worst 10-year results in our 85-year history of stock market prices; by each period's end, most investors who had relied on Smith's or Siegel's message were not happy campers.

If you think I pulled a magician's sleight of hand, giving you something with my right hand—a simple algorithm that could be applied almost by rote—and then quickly removing it with my left hand, you are missing the real message of this book.

Let's get one thing straight. This book is *not* about the 1-year/6-month algorithm. It's about much more. It's about a conceptual investment strategy innovation that uses the knowledge of complex adaptive systems and Darwinian biology as a way to make sense of investment markets.

The algorithm is presented as evidence to make a new investment theory, one that speaks in a language that most readers have not been acquainted with credible. Using the algorithm as proof is much simpler than inventing a new language, as Sir Isaac Newton did when he created the mathematical language of calculus in 1666 in order to make his laws on the motion of the planets more comprehensible. (Gottfried Leibniz actually got the credit for inventing calculus because Newton did not publish his work until much later, though he came up with it 18 years before Leibniz.) I certainly did *not* invent the science of complex adaptive systems; I am just one of the early birds trying to marry it to investing.

Back to the question posed at the beginning of this book: Can we outdistance the S&P 500? And can we do so without the help of our critical mass-finding algorithm? Before we answer, let's take an inventory of what you should be taking away from the book.

HOW MARKETS WORK

First and foremost is a picture of how markets work. Markets are part of a world that operates through a forced human adapattion process (induced through joint market and social mechanisms), which plays out in an oscillating pattern that flips between order and chaos, resulting in a paradox most of us agents (and especially late adapters) fall victim to. This process is an important part of the architecture of complex adaptive systems and is called *punctuated equilibrium*, a long period of stasis wherein the environment appears quite stable (in rough equilibrium), fostering agent complacency. Then some small trigger—we might call it a "Black Swan"—sets off a crisis wherein the system experiences chaotic and revolutionary change. Actually, it sounds like Cato's *snare* reappearing to haunt us once more.

Punctuated Equilibrium

I cannot emphasize enough for readers to familiarize themselves with the concept of punctuated equilibrium, wherein the environment appears to most to be quite stable and not particularly dangerous due to the long period of stasis. Prior periods of destruction and chaos are viewed as historical "outliers," attributed to machinations during an older, less intelligent age.

The concept of punctuated equilibrium sounds much like what happened in the 60 years leading up to mid-2007, wherein, along all frontiers of Western society, we erased the depression of the 1930s, and its effects, from our radar screens. MBA-schooled managers from our most prestigious universities took the captain's seats at most of our large corporations. They were to be assisted by brainy quants who had learned all the new math and the formulas to eliminate risk. All was well in this "New Age"—the world appeared much less dangerous than it really was.

Then amid a pervasive feeling of complacency, several horsemen of the apocalypse mounted up to begin their ride, and by early 2009, people throughout the developed and not-so-developed world shuddered. Millions of American and European families lost their homes; jobs, along with the steady paychecks they provided, disappeared; families' finances were ripped apart; and most Western nations tottered on the edge of a frightening abyss as their underlying financial structures crumbled. Once again, we are in the process of closing the circle of a period of punctuated equilibrium.

Punctuated equilibrium is the enduring architecture of our social world, and it dates back at least to the time of the ancient Greeks. Listen to the words written by an early Greek (Sophocles so far as I can tell):

Not only do men move about on an uncharted landscape.

The landscape itself is in constant motion, and men must

be quick enough to move about with it. When they aren't,

they go through the cracks that open under their feet.

Punctuated equilibrium is still with us; most of us agents are its duped victims.

There is a tendency for people to wed themselves to the particular part of the punctuated equilibrium cycle they came of age in. Usually stasis people are rewarded for patience and perseverance and thus unprepared to deal successfully with the nasty and often brutish periods of rapid revolutionary change. However, those who reach maturity during periods of chaotic change, wherein frequent and volatile changes of direction prevail, find themselves temperamentally ill-suited to flourish during the following calm period of stasis wherein change is mostly incremental. And "adaptive" investors should be aware of this.

MORE TAKE-AWAYS

The second thing I hope you can take away is an appreciation of what an "honest to goodness" bubble looks like and the role it plays in "punctuated equilibrium." Recently there have been many bubble sightings, but only a couple of "true" bubbles. As a reality check, to see if it's the real thing, look for it to be accompanied by an all-pervasive belief that shout's down any doubting skeptics. If it is, expect it to be followed by a long period of disruption and chaos, or a world turned "upside-down."

That said, you should also be aware that if we get too many bubble-spotters, we won't get many (if any) bubbles. The spotters will either not participate in the folly or else sell out when the budding bubble is still in its embryonic stage, way before reaching unrealistic heights. Any true bubble will probably have to await bubble-spotting fatigue.

Yet the flip side of a bubble is what many market observers call capitulation. If a bubble marks the end of a forced march to the upside, capitulation, a pervasive dumping of risk assets, is the tell tale sign that the majority of the agents are concluding their retreat to the downside. Their behavior is becoming markedly risk-averse and will remain so for a fairly long time. Agents become reluctant to own investments, and markets become grossly undervalued.

So far we have had one American major capitulation, the 1930s, and there was another in Japan following the 1980s bubble. Presently the odds seem to favor that we are in the midst of a third such capitulation. While we don't have enough examples yet to draw some boundaries, we can make a tentative guess at a working definition of a capitulation. In both prior capitulations the main index fell by more than 50 percent from its peak, and 10 years, a decade, later the index was *still* below the 50 percent marker, on an inflation-adjusted basis. That's pain, and we can presume a behavioral change, which in time will provide the underpinnings for another march up.

The third thing to take away is an appreciation of the importance of trends. They are the nerve center of the system, as they connect the animating narrative to a behavioral pattern and as such, provide a clear picture of how well we agents are adapting to the emerging new reality. Furthermore, these patterns are often the most important piece of information available, as they tell us in which direction the feedback loops are spinning. The importance of this piece of knowledge is something that most Newtonians simply don't get: Their excessive faith in people's reasoning capacity blinds them to the power of a herdlike pattern to human behavior and its amplifying effect.

The fourth take-away is that evolution and the stock market are smarter than us agents, including both you and me.

Therefore, if we hope to succeed as investors, it would behoove us to replace our Newtonian lenses with Darwinian goggles.

VARIATION AND SELECTION

Take-away number five: the two important Darwinian evolutionary processes, variation and selection.

I gave you four asset class variants. However, in a global economy, wherein a number of emerging markets are growing at breakneck speed, we might, in the future, need more variations to select from. The three most likely possibilities I could think of are commodities, TIPS (Treasury Inflation-Protected Securities), and currencies. But, up until recently, their puny long-term returns couldn't stand up to our big four.

Right now commodities appear to be the best candidate. From the end of 1972 until mid-2002, an index of commodity futures prices has compounded at a puny rate of approximately 3.51. Not very exciting, nor for that matter worthwhile for inclusion in the AIP portfolio. However, since a number of heavily populated developing nations acquired the desire and ability to feed and clothe their citizens, say by approximately mid-2002, the index of commodity prices has compounded at about 7.54 percent (as of March 31, 2011). If that desire and ability to bring large portions of their people to a middle-class lifestyle remains, we could be in for a sustained period of more generous commodity returns.

The case for TIPS rests on the inflationary potential from the immense liquidity that has been injected into banking systems around the world. Currencies, which also suffer from meager long-term compounded returns, would need a huge increase in the volatility between international currencies before we could think of including them. Other possible variants may well surface in the future.

My point is that if you want to think Darwinian, be on the lookout for more variation. I have provided some additional tools to evaluate their potential, via a method to measure the relationship between risk and reward—the gain-to-pain ratio—and a reason (negative correlation) why they should be considered.

In a Darwinian world, the object is to reach into that grab-bag of asset classes and, like "natural selection," select the ones that are good enough "fits" to the prevailing environment. Selection is the second tool borrowed from Darwinian biology. That means designing your very own search engine to look for "fits." When it does "fit," select it; when it doesn't, select a nonrisky alternative in its place. I gave you one such search engine (our 1-year/6-month algorithm, which, by the way, had about a 64 percent rate of success in selecting the best "fit"), but it may no longer be useful. However, I also included a model for constructing an algorithm—including a tilt that made it harder to sell than to buy or vice versa—to identify the critical levels at which a self-organizing trend takes on a life of its own and alerts investors to the likelihood that large parts of the human population will soon follow in a forced adaption march. Some people with pattern-recognizing skills may be able to use the construction methodology to find a new emerging pattern, although the pattern may take a different (non–time price) form.

Your investor job is to select an asset class or a story that fits the changes that are occurring in the crowd's behavioral pattern. And there's one other requirement: You have to do it before most others. If you are able to do this, it means you are probably an early "adapter." This increases your chances, exponentially, to be included at the winner's circle.

Also do not rule out the possibility that there may be other ways than designing an algorithm to find environmental "fits," although these other ways probably will be messier.

THE SYSTEM IS ALSO PART OF THE INVESTMENT PUZZLE

The sixth and final take-away: There is the great unknown. That is the part that the system which we all belong to plays in the investment puzzle. Living systems have their own life spans, much like other biological living things. What we agents, with our knowledge limitations, don't and can't know, is where our wealth-generating system is on its "life" cycle clock. Is the system in a vigorous youth stage, wherein an overabundance of energy provides a robust performance? Or in a mature phase, characterized by stability and a respectable performance? Or how about a doddering old-age stage, wherein energy is seeping out and performance is well below par and iffy? Systems, like other life forms, often become less vigorous as they age.

CAN THE MARKET BE BEAT?

So "Can the market be beat?" The answer is a qualified Yes, but only for a minority, as we all can't beat a crowd we are part of.

Oh, and one last thing, before I close (as food for thought), investment markets appear to be the great game of uncertainty—they are, perhaps, smaller, more concise versions of the larger game of life, providing insights into the historical process, and as such, they may well be the prime place (the Galapagos) to learn about "how our world works."

In closing, I want you, Dear Reader, to know I've given you my best. Now you have to take it from here.

Notes

Preface

1. Eric D. Beinhocker, *The Origin of Wealth*, Cambridge, MA: Harvard Business Press, 2007.

Chapter 1

1. John J. Raskob, as interviewed by Samuel Crowther, "Everybody Ought to Be Rich," *Ladies Home Journal*, 1929.
2. "The Death of Equities: How Inflation Is Destroying the Stock Market," *Business Week*, August 13, 1979. Available at http://www. businessweek. com/investor/content/mar2009/pi20090310_263462.htm
3. Clyde V. Prestowitz Jr., *Trading Places: How We Allowed Japan to Take the Lead*, New York: Basic Books, 1988.

Chapter 2

1. Eleanor Laise, "Bruised Quant Funds Seek a Human Touch," *Wall Street Journal*, September 2, 2010. Available online at http://online.wsj.com/article/SB10001424052748703649004575437290148983902.html?mod=WSJ_PersonalFinance_PF2#

Chapter 3

1. Quotation cited in *Encylopaedia Brittanica*.

Chapter 5

1. Jeremy Siegel, *Stocks for the Long Run: The Definitive Guide to Financial Market Returns and Long Term Investment Strategies*, 4th ed. New York: McGraw-Hill, 2007.

Chapter 7

1. John Maynard Keynes, *General Theory of Employment, Interest, and Money*. Eastford, CT: Martino Publishing, 2011, p. 124.
2. David Leonhardt, "A Forecast with Hope Built In," *New York Times*, June 30, 2009. Available at http://www.nytimes.com/ 2009/07/01/ business/01leonhardt.html?scp=1&sq=A%20Forecast%20with%20 Hope%20Built%20In&st=cse

Chapter 8

1. Lawrence McDonald and Patrick Robinson, *A Colossal Failure of Common Sense: The Inside Story of the Collapse of Lehman Brothers*. New York: Crown, 2010.
2. James K. Glassman and Kevin A. Hassett, *Dow 36,000: The New Strategy for Profiting from the Coming Rise in the Stock Market*. New York: Times Books, 1999.
3. John Trenchard and Thomas Gordon, eds. *Cato's Letters*, Vol. 1, "Letter No. 13." Indianapolis: Liberty Fund Publishing, 1995. Originally published ca. 1720–1721.
4. Edgar Lawrence Smith, *Common Stocks as Long-Term Investments*. Reissue. Whitefish, MT: Kessinger Publishing, 2003.
5. From Nikos Kazantzakis, *The Last Temptation*. New York: Simon & Schuster, 1960.

Chapter 10

1. The slight discrepancy between this 16.04 compounded return and the earlier 16.03 number from Table 5–1 is due to rounding differences.

Chapter 14

1. Edgar Lawrence Smith, *Stocks as Long-Term Investments*. Reissue. Whitefish, MT: Kessinger Publishing, 2003.

Chapter 16

1. Paul Ehrlich, *The Population Bomb*. New York: Sierra Club-Ballantine, 1970.
2. Carmen Reinhardt and Kenneth Rogoff, *This Time Is Different: Eight Centuries of Financial Folly*. Princeton, NJ: Princeton University Press, 2009.

Index

ER of, 128
G/P ratio of, 128
risk in, 42–43
standard deviation of, 128
strategy of, 38–39, 80, 210

Cabdriver, 203–205
Capital appreciation, 182–183
Capital gains, 47
Capitalism. *See also* Free market system
  economy of, 27–28
  free-market, 1, 7, 83, 105
  punctuated equilibrium in, 38
Capitulation, 229
CAS. *See* Complex adaptive systems
Case, Karl, 179
Case-Shiller National Real Estate Index
    (CSI), 149, 179–182
  unleveraged, levered 5:1, levered 2.5:1
    and, 184–186
Casey, Douglas, 7
Castro, Fidel, 204–205
Cato's snare, 103–105, 227
Cause and effect logic, 4, 10, 25–26,
    32–34, 108
Central Powers, 202
Chamberlain, Neville, 198
Change, rapid, 30, 32, 37, 227–228
Channel breakout method,
    115–117
China, 42
Civilizations, 39–41
Clinton, Bill, 33, 213
Closing prices, 115
Club of Rome, 211
CMPD. *See* Compounded returns
Cognitive dissonance, 196
Cohen, Abby Joseph, 96
Cohen & Steers, 144
College student, 203–205
A Colossal Failure of Common Sense
    (McDonald), 97
Combined investment A/B portfolio,
    67–69
Commodities, 230
Common Stocks as Long-Term Investments
    (Smith, E.), 104
Communist, 204, 205
Competition, 30
Complex adaptive systems (CAS),
    25–28, 81
  bubbles in, 215
  critical levels in, 115–117, 223
  errors in, 106–108

investment strategies and, 226
  political role in, 220–221
Compounded returns (CMPD), 17, 18, 20
Consumer price index (CPI), 48–52, 54
Corrections, 89
Corruption, 102
Countertrend, 89
Cowles Foundation for Research in
    Economics, 182
CPI. *See* Consumer price index
Credit, 48
  bubble territory related to, 96
  cut backs, 136
  real estate bubble related to, 100–102
Crises
  of 1929, 38, 103–105, 183
  of 1987, 19
  of 2008, 19, 23, 38, 91, 213
  developing plan in event of, 175–177
  food shortage, 211
  forecasting and, 85
  global warming, 211
  S&L, 211, 212–213
  strategies during, 42–43
CRISP database, 11
Critical level, 87, 89, 92–93, 111
  in CAS systems, 115–117, 223
  in stock market, 115–117
Critical level-search method. *See* Buy
    and sell method
CSI. *See* Case-Shiller National Real
    Estate Index
Cuba, 204–205
Culture, in investment community,
    87–88, 90
Currencies, 230
Cyclical pattern, of fluctuating markets,
    83–86

Daladier, Edouard, 198
Darwin, Charles, 28, 30
Darwinian thinking, 24, 34–35, 81
  decision making and, 199–200, 203
Data
  mining, 116, 117
  value pertaining to, 84–86
Day traders, 98–99
DDs. *See* Drawdowns
Debt, 89, 102, 219
Decision making, 26, 195–196
  in 1930s, 197–199, 201–202
  Darwinian thinking and, 199–200, 203
  faulty, 196–197, 202–203, 208
  process/outcome related to, 206–207